You Can Be The Wife of A Happy Husband

DARIEN B. COOPER

Chariot VICTOR
PUBLISHING
A DIVISION OF COOK COMMUNICATIONS

ChariotVICTOR Publishing,
a division of Cook Communications, Colorado Springs, Colorado 80918
Cook Communications, Paris, Ontario
Kingsway Communications, Eastbourne, England

51   52   53   54   64   Printing/Year   99   98

Library of Congress Catalog Card No. 74-77450

ISBN 1-56476-711-6

DARIEN COOPER is the wife of DeWitt, a construction contractor when this book was written. They have three sons—Craig, Brian, and Ken. A resident of Decatur, Ga., Mrs. Cooper is known in many Southern cities for her women's Bible classes and lectures. Her series "You Can Be the Wife of a Happy Husband" has been a source of great help to those women who have put into practice the biblical principles that Darien teaches. Many wives speak of transformed marriages. Says one, "Application of these truths has brought me closer to my husband than we've been in eleven years of marriage. He thanks you too."

A graduate of Carson Newman College, Jefferson City, Tenn., with a B.A. in sociology, Darien Cooper hoped to help others find solutions to life's problems. Though she passed the state board social work examination, circumstances prevented her entering that field.

Some years later, while serving temporarily with her husband on the associate staff of the Lay Ministry of Campus Crusade for Christ, Darien learned biblical principles that completely changed her own life and marriage. "We were growing apart until God enabled me to apply these truths to my life," she says. DeWitt was so impressed that he encouraged her to begin teaching a course "on the truths that changed our marriage."

The "Happy Husband" lecture series has been intensively reworked and put into print in these pages in the hope that you will find God's greatest happiness by applying His principles to your marriage. Though the book is designed for your individual help and enrichment, it is ideal for group study as well. Leader's guides are available.

A cassette course and workbook based on this book, and other subjects by the author, are available by writing His Way Library, P.O. Box 950, Rocky Face, GA 30740.

*Dedicated
to
my beloved
DeWitt*

Contents

A
SPECIAL TRIBUTE
to
Patricia Bradley
and Grace Fox
to whom
*I am deeply indebted for their endless
hours of work, revising, clarifying,
and criticizing my writing to make
this book possible. They considered
their contributions an honor and a privilege.
Their attitudes have been an
inspiration to me.*

Foreword

In a day when almost every newspaper in the country gives front page space to the inane, harmful pronouncements of the women's libbers, it is refreshing to hear an attractive, godly woman speak up. Darien Cooper is a real woman—satisfied and fulfilled. It did not take her three or four marriages to discover what it takes to please a man. She discovered that secret the first time around and is practicing what she teaches.

Four men love and admire this young woman: her husband and their three sons. Hundreds of women attend her two weekly Bible classes, where she expounds the principles found in this book. Many troubled wives have been brought into her classes by friends and have gone away transformed by the principles Mrs. Cooper teaches. A number of these women have changed from competitor to partner, much to the amazement of their husbands.

I first met Darien when I went to Atlanta, Ga., to hold a Family Life Seminar. She and her husband, DeWitt, met my wife and me at the Atlanta airport. I was excited when I heard how God was using Darien in the much needed area of developing feminine contentment in the home through teaching biblical principles. But I was even more impressed with the way her husband shared her enthusiasm about her ministry.

Any time I find a man who takes genuine pride in what his wife does outside the home, I know she must be a wise woman. It's natural for a man to feel threatened by his partner's success. Not so with DeWitt. He is thrilled that God is using Darien to help wives experience satisfying relationships with their husbands.

It is about time a woman says some of the things Darien expresses in this book. She has an excellent grasp of the biblical concepts that produce happiness in marriage and states them clearly. She knows that a woman is not some weak, frilly, brainless creature man marries only for erotic pleasure or to display as an ornament. Instead, she sees a woman as an absolute essential to a man's fulfillment in life. But she is vitally aware that a wife must accept her God-given role or she will ruin the partnership.

Darien Cooper has a thorough understanding of the male ego. In this book she discusses the biblical principles every wife needs to know in order to live with that ego. Many family explosions could be avoided if more wives knew these secrets. Hopefully, thousands of women who may never have a chance to hear Darien speak will read this book and find God's help for their marriages.

TIM LaHaye

Introduction

You can find your true identity by discovering God's role for you as a woman and a wife. This book is designed to help you make those discoveries.

I believe God has given us women the choice role. Unfortunately, many of us do not realize that being a woman and a wife is a wonderful privilege, so we miss the joy and fulfillment God has in store for us. Though we want happiness, some of us back off after being exposed to the biblical principles and concepts explained in this book. We say, "This is too good to be true," or "It won't work for me," or as I once said, "You've got to be kidding. I don't need help."

At that time I wasn't teachable. Had you asked me if I had any problems personally, I would have replied, "Nothing serious; nothing that needs changing. But my husband—now that's something else!"

I thought I had a good marriage, but as I look back now, I realize I simply had a good man. For 12 years I tried to change DeWitt—the way he did things or didn't do them, or the way he related to me.

I tried direct approaches and subtle ones. I'd cry when he forgot my birthday or our anniversary. I wondered why he wouldn't come and put his arms around me and tell me he was sorry and loved me. But it seemed as if the more I cried, the less attention he gave me.

One day I said, "DeWitt, I've been watching the Joneses next door. Mr. Jones is so thoughtful. He brings his wife candy and flowers. He always kisses her affectionately at the door when he comes home from work. I wonder why you don't do that?"

"Because I don't know her that well," he responded.

I'd listen to what he'd tell me when he came home from work, and give him advice as to what he should or should not have said or done. I couldn't understand why he didn't seem to appreciate my advice and stopped sharing with me.

Then about six years ago, after an intensive study of the Bible, I saw that God had definite solutions to life's problems. And a detailed outline of how a successful marriage should be maintained. I realized that instead of helping DeWitt, I was crushing him—destroying his masculinity. I said, "OK, God, I'm ready for You to show me how to be the kind of wife I should be."

Today, I am enjoying the kind of fulfilling relationship God meant each marriage to be. Life is exciting since I've applied the principles God gave me in the Bible. I've found that I can have complete peace and satisfaction in my marriage, regardless of circumstances.

God is no respecter of persons. His truth is for all who believe and trust Him by obeying His Word. All you need is a teachable attitude—the willingness to let God work in your life. As you trust God and obey His Word, you will find—as I did and as so many other women have—the fulfillment you want.

I have written this book in order to share with as many women as possible the truths that have transformed my life and marriage over the last six years. The only regret I have is that I did not know these principles sooner.

It is important that you read the book in the sequence in which it is written, since each chapter builds on the previous one. Please reserve judgment of any single truth presented until you've read the whole book and have the overall picture. And as you study these principles, remember that they apply whether or not your husband is a believer in Jesus Christ.

As you put these principles into practice and make them

10

a way of life, you should see changes in your husband as well as yourself. It is exciting to hear and see the reactions of husbands who don't know that their wives are studying God's plan for a happy marriage relationship. Many cannot understand why their wives have suddenly become sweeter or easier to live with.

But changes take time, so be patient and let God do the changing. Rely on Him to build or rebuild your marriage. "Except the Lord builds the house, they labor in vain who build it" (Psalm 127:1).

May I suggest that you begin a personal notebook. As you read this book, jot down in one column attitudes and habits in your life that need to be changed. Ask God to show you creative steps you can take to change each wrong attitude or habit. List these steps in the opposite column. Then, as God leads, try these ideas out. You will be encouraged as you look back later and see the changes God has made in your life.

It is my prayer that through this book, you will discover the full, satisfying life God has for you as a woman and a wife, and that you'll become the wife your husband needs. To put it another way, you will become "the wife of a happy husband."

I want to express deep appreciation to the many people whose dedicated help has made this book possible: My husband DeWitt and three sons, Craig, Brian, and Ken, made writing easier because of their enthusiastic cooperation. Mrs. Willis Horton patiently taught me many of these truths. Phyllis Ott typed the manuscript and gave helpful suggestions. Anna Stanley gave me the idea of writing this book. And, finally, I appreciate the scores of women who have permitted me to tell their experiences as illustrations—disguised, of course, to conceal identities.

1

The Perfect Plan

One warm afternoon several years ago in Valdosta, Georgia, Margie Maultsby, an attractive black woman in her thirties, was seriously planning her future apart from her husband, Joe. Though they had been reunited for six months following a separation she had forced, their life together was not any better.

The next day a casual acquaintance invited her to attend a neighborhood Bible class featuring my cassette messages on the biblical principles contained in this book. But Margie had no intention of going. After all, what could a white woman possibly offer her to help her hopeless marriage?

Nevertheless, God knew her need, and drew her to the class. Her letters to God written after the first and second sessions reveal her heart:

DEAR GOD,
Can You believe I attended that Bible class? Don't ask me why! Before I knew anything, I was ringing that doorbell, introducing myself to the Bible-class leader, hostess, and taking a seat among ten other strangers.

Did I enjoy the class? I don't know; I can't remember too much. However, I do have homework. This is ludicrous; I have enough schoolwork to do as it is. After all, Father, I am an English teacher. I really don't have time for this; I probably won't go again. That lady on the cassette tape can't tell me anything that I don't know. I've read lots of material on marriages. I'm still trying to apply some of those principles. My marriage is okay anyway. It's about as good as most. Everybody has problems. Anyway, I don't want to think about marriage; I want to think about You and Christ.

MARGIE

DEAR GOD,
I'm still in a state of shock after last night in that ladies Bible class! Yes, I went again!

Well, I received quite a blow; it was truly a bolt! I discovered that I didn't really love my husband. Can You believe this? I couldn't. I thought I had always been a good wife. However, when I began to listen to the words from 1 Corinthians 13:4-7 for the first time, those words describing love began to have some merit—is kind, not jealous, thinks no evil, seeks not her own, believes all things, hopes all things, endures all things. I realized that I am kind to Joe only when he does what I want him to do. I've got a lot to learn!

You see, God, I am actually jealous! At night, I search Joe's wallet. I also check his stories when he comes home so that I can make sure that he is telling the truth. How else would I know? Sometimes I wait up for him just to attack him with threatening words and accusations. At these times, I am constantly thinking evil. I have looked at Joe for so long; I had no idea that my mirror held so much evil.

In addition to all that has been said, Heavenly Father, I seek my own way. I never really give any thought to Joe's dreams; I'm only interested in mine. I never let him be free to think, to plan, or to dream. I try only to make my values his values.

You see, Joe, belongs to a club, and I'm always afraid that if he behaves badly at a night club or if he stays out too late that someone may think less of me or even less of my marriage. Stupid, I know. However, for this reason, I have always tried to get him to watch his behavior. Not only is this wrong according to Your Word, but it doesn't work anyway. If I lecture for a long time or if I become angry and threaten to leave him, he does seem to behave according to my standards for a while.

During these times, I am on top of the world. Then . . . boom! back to his same old habits. I should have known something was wrong, but I didn't. I thought this was just the way to live. Then I read, "Except the Lord build the house, they labor in vain who build it" (Ps. 127:1). I give You my house to build. Father, teach me how to love my husband.

MARGIE

After the second class, Margie placed her life and her marriage completely in God's hands. The next year was very difficult, but Jesus gave her the strength to love Joe unconditionally. Shortly thereafter, she was rewarded when Joe, with much tenderness and a new consideration for her, said, "I want the Lord to give me a portion of what you have."

Margie died to her old ways. In turn, she was free to love God's way. She and Joe are now enjoying a new love for each other and a marital fulfillment that God wants to give to all couples. God is now using Margie mightly to teach others in Decatur, Georgia, where she now lives.

A Satisfying Life

God did not create you and put you on this earth to live an apathetic, frustrated, defeated, or discouraged life. He meant you to be happier than you ever dreamed possible. "Now glory be to God who by His mighty power at work within us is able to do far more than we would ever dare to ask to even dream of— infinitely beyond our highest prayers, desires, thoughts, or hopes'' (Ephesians 3:20, LB). Jesus Christ said that He came to provide a satisfying, complete life for you. "I came that they may have and enjoy life, and have it in abundance to the full, till it overflows" (John 10:10).

This life is available to you regardless of your background, education, nationality, or present circumstances. There is no problem too large or too small for Christ to work out in your life. All that He requires from you is a willing heart and obedience to His plan. "If you are willing and obedient, you shall eat the good of the land" (Isaiah 1:19). The "good of the land" can be compared to an abundant life for you.

A Personalized Plan
God loves you so much that He has worked out a personal plan for you to experience growth, development, and fulfillment. You should think of your life as a divine prescription from the hand of God. "You made all the delicate, inner parts of my body, and knit them together in my mother's womb. Thank You for making me so wonderfully complex! It is amazing to think about.

"Your workmanship is marvelous—and how well I know it. You were there while I was being formed in utter seclusion! You saw me before I was born and scheduled each day of my life before I began to breathe. Every day was recorded in Your Book! How precious it is, Lord, to realize that you are thinking about me constantly! I can't even count how many times a day Your thoughts turn towards me. And when I waken in the morning, You are still thinking of me!" (Psalm 139:13-18, LB)

God cares so much for you that He is always thinking about you and watching everything that concerns you. No accidents occur in the lives of God's children. He desires to use your personality, your physical makeup, and your background to your advantage.

If you trust Him, He can take all of the things in your life that you would like to change and work them out for your good. "We are assured and know that [God being a partner in their labor], all things work together and are [fitting into a plan] for good to those who love God and are called according to [His] design and purpose" (Romans 8:28). Notice that He did not say that all things *are good,* but that He would *work all things out for your good.* Only God can perform such miracles.

Do not question what God is doing; simply trust Him to know what is best for you. "But who are you, a mere man, to criticize and contradict and answer back to God? Will what is formed say to Him that formed it, 'Why have You made me thus?' " (Romans 9:20) This means that you are not to question why you are the way you are or why your husband is as he is. Rather, you are to discover and accept God's plan for your life so that He can work out all things to your advantage.

Marriage—A Fulfilling Relationship

Everything God has designed for you is for your benefit. Thus, marriage was designed by God to give you the greatest human happiness possible. This relationship is described in Ephesians 5:21-33: "Be subject to one another out of reverence for Christ, the Messiah, the Anointed One. Wives, be subject—be submissive and adapt yourselves—to your own husbands as [a service] to the Lord. For the husband is head of the wife as Christ is the Head of the Church, Himself the Saviour of [His] body. As the Church is subject to Christ, so let wives also be subject in everything to their husbands.

"Husbands, love your wives, as Christ loved the Church and gave Himself up for her. . . . Even so husbands should love their wives as [being in a sense] their own bodies. He who loves his own wife loves himself. For no man ever hated his own flesh, but nourishes and carefully protects and cherishes it, as Christ does the Church. . . . For this reason a man shall leave his father and his mother and shall be joined to his wife, and the two shall become one flesh. . . . However, let each man of you (without exception) love his wife as [being in a sense] his very own self; and let the wife see that she respects and reverences her husband.''

I believe the role of the wife in the marital relationship is the choice role. She is to be loved, protected, and cherished by her husband in the same way that Christ gave Himself for the Church (believers). The words ''be subject'' or ''be submissive'' describe the way you are to relate to your husband. Another way of saying it is that you are to be a *responder* to your husband's love, protection, and leadership. Submission never means that your personality, abilities, talents, or individuality are buried, but that they will be channeled to operate to the maximum.

Someone said, ''Woman was created from man, not from his head to be commanded by him, nor from his feet to be his slave. Rather, she was taken from his side to complement him, near his arms to be protected by him, and close to his heart to be loved.'' Submission never imprisons you. It liberates you, giving you the freedom to be creative under the protection of divinely appointed authority.

Wasn't your relationship before marriage one of your responding to his love and leadership? He expressed his love and leadership by being thoughtful, complimenting you, and bringing you gifts. You responded to this love by making yourself attractive to please him or by going places with him that you may not have really cared about simply because you enjoyed his company.

Then, after marriage things began to change. What happened? Could it be that you gradually left your role of responder by no longer taking time to look your best for your husband or refusing to share his interests? Yes, it is easy to stop responding to your husband without even realizing it.

A wise woman knows that she cannot take her role lightly but must seriously work at building a lasting, fulfilling relationship. "Every wise woman builds her house, but the foolish one tears it down with her own hands" (Proverbs 14:1). A woman can act foolishly and destroy her marriage, yet not be aware that she is violating principles that build a successful marriage. That is the reason women must be taught "to love their husbands and their children; to be self-controlled, chaste, homemakers, good-natured (kindhearted), adapting and subordinating themselves to their husbands, that the Word of God may not be exposed to reproach—blasphemed or discredited" (Titus 2:4-5).

Because the world has done an effective job of distorting the marriage relationship and its respective roles, the foolish woman often feels unfulfilled. She is convinced that her unhappiness is caused by her homemaking and child care responsibilities. She seeks fulfillment in trying to change her role through such means as the women's liberation movement. Actually, though her unhappiness is not a result of her role but of her failure to understand and fulfill the role God designed for her.

The wise woman recognizes God's principles for building a successful marriage and applies them. She realizes that a successful marriage requires planning in the same way any successful venture does. For instance, in baking a light, delicious cake, she must put in the right ingredients at the right time, in the proper proportions. The same is true of a marriage. In order to develop a happy marriage, the truly wise woman will use the proper principles, at the right time, with a divine balance. A good marriage does not just happen. It is deliberately built through the years.

The Book of Esther gives examples of both the foolish and wise woman. Queen Vashti, the foolish woman, did not respond to her husband's leadership when he requested that she join the party he was giving and let his guests observe her beauty. As a result, she was banished from the king's presence, and he chose Esther to be his queen.*

Esther, a wise woman, responded to King Ahasuerus' leadership and the results were wonderful! During a period of crisis when she could have lost her life, her submissive attitude and wise actions caused the king to say, "Now tell me what you really want, and I will give it to you, even if it is half of the kingdom!" (Esther 5:6, LB) The crisis was over. Esther's life and the lives of her people were saved because of right and wise actions on her part.

A wise woman will build a successful marriage by meeting her husband's needs in the manner described in Proverbs 31:12: "She will comfort, encourage and do him only good as long as there is life within her."

Use this verse as a measuring stick to determine our own attitudes or actions. Ask yourself, "How can I comfort, encourage, or do my husband good?" Sometimes this may mean comforting him when his boss has given him a hard day at work or encouraging him when he begins to doubt his ability to provide for his family. As you act wisely, you will see a miraculous blossoming of your marriage relationship.

---

*Even though some Christians believe that Queen Vashti was asked to perform some lewd act and was therefore justified in her disobedience, there is nothing in the Hebrew text or the customs of the Persians to indicate that she was asked to commit a sin.

2

Your Relationship with the Designer

The need for a woman was evident in the life of the first man. Adam was created perfect by the Lord and placed in a perfect environment, the Garden of Eden. There, he had fellowship with God and an interesting occupation. Yet he needed a counterpart—someone who could meet his human needs.

So God provided the woman. "Now the Lord God said, 'It is not good [sufficient, satisfactory] that the man should be alone; I will make him a helper meet (suitable, adapted, completing) for him.' Then Adam said, 'This [creature] is now bone of my bones, and flesh of my flesh. She shall be called Woman, because she was taken out of a man' " (Genesis 2:18, 23).

Because God made woman, she was perfect. Her beauty must have been beyond anything we can imagine. Adam took one look at her and saw immediately that she was different from him, yet was his counterpart.

The New Testament echoes man's need for the woman and God's purpose in making her. "The man wasn't made from the woman but the woman from man, and the man wasn't made for the woman but the woman for the man" (1 Corinthians 11:8-9, BECK). One beautiful aspect of God's plan is that the woman will find happiness herself as she meets her husband's needs.

A woman can also have tremendous influence on her husband because of her special abilities to meet those needs.

When the first woman left her role of responding to her husband's leadership, she made a grave mistake which affected all mankind (see Genesis 3:1-6). Eve allowed Satan's subtle conversation and deceit to influence her thinking and cause her to doubt that God's plan was for her good. Once she doubted God's complete love and provision, it was not long before she sinned—acted independently of God and His plan for her life.

Having made the mistake herself, Eve used her influence to draw her husband into the same mistake. "And she gave some also to her husband, and he ate" (Genesis 3:6). She gave and he ate! According to 1 Timothy 2:13-14, Adam was not deceived. He knew what he was doing. He had a choice between continuing in perfect fellowship with the Lord or joining his beloved wife in her fallen state. Knowing the consequences, he chose a fallen state with Eve rather than be without her. Yes, the influence of a woman is tremendous.

If you aren't trusting God for guidance, you may influence your husband in the wrong way. An account is given in Genesis 16 of Sarai (later called Sarah), a godly woman, who left her role of responding to her husband's leadership and influenced him in a way she later regretted. Many years had passed since God had promised them a son. Sarai became impatient and tried to help God fulfill His promise by giving her maid to her husband so the maid might bear them a son.

Sarai stepped out of the role God had designed for her and took matters into her own hands, thus influencing her husband to sin. This sin is causing and has caused pain for many people through the centuries as the children of Hagar and Sarai have warred against each other. Woman's role is a big responsibility as well as a wonderful privilege.

Woman's Need

Before the fall of man (see Genesis 3), woman was complete in body, soul, and spirit. Each day she enjoyed fellowship with the Lord and her husband. When she disobeyed God and ate the fruit of the tree of the knowledge of good and evil, she died as God had said she would. She did not die physically for several hundred years, but she died spiritually at once. Her human spirit, the part of her that could understand God's truths and enjoy His fellowship, died then. Immediately, there was an emptiness in her life that could be filled only by regaining a personal relationship with God Himself.

It has been said that "there is a God-shaped vacuum in the heart of each person which cannot be filled by anything or anyone but God, the Creator, made known through Jesus Christ." Each member of the human race comes into this world in the same fallen state in which Eve found herself immediately after her sin. The old sin nature has been transmitted to each of us through Adam. "Therefore as sin came into the world through one man and death as the result of sin, so death spread to all men, [no one being able to stop it or to escape its power] because all men sinned" (Romans 5:12).

Figure A in the following drawings illustrates our condition when we come into the world. Each of us has a control center in her life. Without Christ in our lives, the old sin nature (self—I—flesh—old man—or whatever term you use) is controlling us. This sin nature shows up clearly in children. We don't have to teach them to be selfish or to demand their own way. They do that naturally. The old sin nature is selfish and demanding.

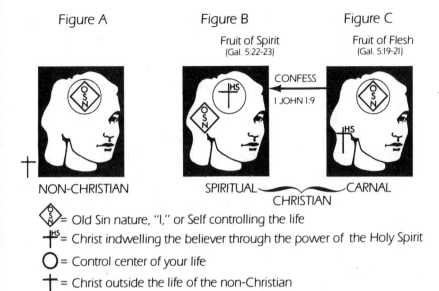

Figure A

Figure B

Fruit of Spirit
(Gal. 5:22-23)

Figure C

Fruit of Flesh
(Gal. 5:19-21)

CONFESS

1 JOHN 1:9

NON-CHRISTIAN

SPIRITUAL

CARNAL

CHRISTIAN

= Old Sin nature, "I," or Self controlling the life

= Christ indwelling the believer through the power of the Holy Spirit

O = Control center of your life

† = Christ outside the life of the non-Christian

God loved you so much He designed a plan whereby you could be restored to fellowship with Him without compromising His own perfect character. (The barrier of sin between you and God had to be removed before God could express His love for you since His righteousness could not tolerate contact with sin. God, being perfectly just, could not overlook your sin but required that the penalty—death—be paid.) Jesus, who is God's Son, accomplished the Father's plan by leaving the glories of heaven to come to earth. He was born into the human race, adding humanity to His deity. By living a perfect life and willingly dying on the cross to pay the penalty for our sins, He provided for our salvation. "He made Him who knew no sin to be sin on our behalf, that we might become the righteousness of God in Him" (2 Corinthians 5:21, NASB).

While Jesus hung there on the cross for three hours, the Father "caused the iniquity of us all to fall on Him" (Isaiah

53:6, NASB). Jesus paid the full price for your sins less than 2,000 years ago, for your every sin—past, present, and future. He said, "It is finished" (John 19:30). He did all the work necessary to provide your salvation. You cannot earn or deserve it. It is a free gift which you must receive before it belongs to you.

It is important that you realize that your sin has been dealt with, regardless of how great you feel it is. The issue is, "Will you accept or reject Jesus Christ's work for you on the cross?" (See John 3:18.) There is no way to know God except through His Son. That is why Jesus said, "I am the Way, and the Truth, and the Life; no one comes to the Father, but through Me" (John 14:6, NASB). When you accept His work on the cross for you, personally, you become God's child.

If you're not sure right now that you are God's child, a member of His forever family, why don't you make sure? The Bible says that you can *know* you are God's child once you have received His Son. "God has given us eternal life, and this life is in His Son. He who has the Son has the life; he who does not have the Son of God does not have the life. These things I have written to you who believe in the name of the Son of God, in order that you may *know that you have eternal life*" (1 John 5:11-13, NASB).

Right now, in the silence of your own heart, you can tell the Father that you do accept His perfect gift of salvation by receiving His Son as your personal Saviour. You can know that you are His child on the basis of His Word, not by what you do or feel.

When you, whether just now or in the past, trusted Jesus Christ to come into your life, you moved to the condition represented by Figure B (p. 23). Jesus Christ came into your life through the renewing power of the Holy Spirit, and you became a child of God. At that moment the Holy Spirit came to live in you so you could live a Christian life (see Romans 8:9). Just as you could not die to pay for your own sins, neither can you, yourself, live the Christian life. Jesus Christ wants to relive His life in you and through you, moment by moment, if you will allow Him. As you trust in His victory over sin for you at the cross, the old sin nature in you is rendered helpless or inactive.

Because of Christ's victory over sin, you no longer have to panic when things go wrong. You know those days when Johnny and Jim begin a fight and, just as you are trying to settle it, the phone rings, then something boils over on the stove? You can have real control and peace through such times by drawing on Jesus' strength instead of your own. He promises to be sufficient (see 2 Corinthians 9:8). Not only that, He says He will use just such irritations as these to shape or mold you into the image of His Son Jesus Christ (see Romans 8:29).

It is as if you are a diamond in the rough being made into the image of Jesus Christ by the Master Craftsman. Each day can become an adventure if you think of its joys and trials as part of God's process of shaping you into a divine original. You can relax, trusting His skilled craftsmanship. "He has made us what we are, because He has created us through our union with Christ Jesus for doing good deeds" (Ephesians 2:10, WMS).

Even though you are God's child, it is possible for you to again take control of your life and feel frustrated and dissatisfied. Figure C (p. 23) pictures this condition. Paul describes it as follows: "I don't understand myself at all, for I really want to do what is right, but I can't. I do what I don't want to—what I hate. I know perfectly well that what I am doing is wrong, and my bad conscience proves that I agree with these laws I am breaking. But I can't help myself, because I'm no longer doing it. It is sin inside me that is stronger than

I am that makes me do these evil things.

"I know I am rotten through and through so far as my old sinful nature [OSN] is concerned. No matter which way I turn I can't make myself do right. I want to, but I can't. When I want to do good, I don't; and when I try not to do wrong, I do it anyway. Now if I am doing what I don't want to, it is plain where the trouble is: sin still has me in its evil grasp. . . . So you see how it is: my new life tells me to do right, but the old nature that is still inside me loves to sin.

"Oh, what a terrible predicament I'm in! Who will free me from my slavery to this deadly lower nature? Thank God! It has been done by Jesus Christ, our Lord. He has set me free" (Romans 7:15-25, LB).

Worry, jealousy, discouragement, a critical attitude, and bitterness are symptoms that you are controlling your own life. Recognize these symptoms as sin and claim the promise in 1 John 1:9 (KJV): "If we confess our sins, He is faithful and just to forgive us our sins, and to cleanse us from all unrighteousness." Then by faith, know you are filled and controlled by the Holy Spirit and back in the condition described in Figure B. (See Colossians 2:6 and Ephesians 5:18.)

Remember that Jesus Christ is a Gentleman. He will not come into your life against your will, nor does He take control of your life without your permission. However, once you've invited Him into your life, He promises never to leave you (see Hebrews 13:5).

Both Christianity and marriage involve a deliberate choice. You choose to commit your total person—intellect, emotions, and will to another. When I met DeWitt, intellectually I liked what I saw—looks, personality, and many other qualities. Yet there is more to marriage than respect and admiration. As we became better acquainted, cupid found his mark. But our loving each other didn't make us married. We became engaged and the wedding day arrived. Intellectually, I believed that he was the most wonderful man in all of the world. Emotionally, my heart beat twice as fast when we were together. But something more took place. In exchanging our vows before the minister, we committed our wills to each other. It was this act of committing our entire selves—intellect, emotions, and will—to each other that made us truly married. The same is true in Christianity. Through a deliberate committing of your will, you become a member of God's family. Both commitments are designed to enable you to be a complete, fulfilled woman.

As Christ meets your personal needs, you can, in turn, meet your husband's needs by following the pattern given in 1 Corinthians 7:34: "But the married woman has her cares [centered] in earthly affairs, how she may please her husband." Begin doing the things for your husband that you know will please him. Sew on that button he has been talking about for so long. Have supper on time. Enjoy a ball game with him. Bake the pie he loves, or train the children to remove their bicycles from the driveway before he comes home. Make it a point to fulfill your husband's desires for you and the children. As you do, you will find that your marriage relationship will take on new meaning.

3
Accepting Your Husband as He Is

The most important gift from God is a personal relationship with Jesus Christ. For the married woman, His next most important gift is her marriage. It is a relationship God created and honors. As she responds to her husband in the way God means her to, she can expect God to bless her.

Marriage—Wonderful Gift or Surprise Package
You may have thought when you received your "gift" that it was perfect. But after the exchange of "I do's," when you began to unwrap your package, the gift turned out to be a surprise. You may have even decided that you had the wrong husband. It's important to realize that, even though you did not know exactly what you were getting, God did.

One wonderful thing about God is that He does not fail. If you trust Him, He will take all things and work them out for your good (see Romans 8:28). He can use the very thing in your husband that you dislike most to mold you into the image of Christ. He wants you to settle down to a lifetime of enjoying the gift you promised to honor and cherish.

What Acceptance Involves

You learn to accept others, including your husband, by noticing how Christ accepts you: "While we were yet sinners, Christ died for us" (Romans 5:8, KJV). God loves and accepts you unconditionally. You are not on probation with Him. Unconditional love and acceptance, then, should be the basis of your marriage.

At times, you may feel that it is asking too much of you to accept your husband as he is. But I guarantee that as you begin to accept him, you will develop a more meaningful relationship with him because both of you will have the freedom you need to mature.

When you accept your husband the way he is, you will give him the freedom to be the man he wants to be. He will have freedom to come and go as he pleases and to make his own decisions. In other words, true love is letting go! Your husband will love you freely as he did when he chose to marry you unless you stifle that love with your possessiveness.

A plant needs water, sun, and fresh air, with room to spread its roots in order to grow and be healthy. Even so, a man needs unconditional love, freedom, and acceptance in order to love and cherish you as God meant him to. As you love your husband unconditionally—without demands and ultimatums—you will see him drawn to you like steel to a magnet.

True love is beautifully described in 1 Corinthians 13:4-7: "Love endures long and is patient and kind; love never is envious nor boils over with jealousy; is not boastful or vainglorious, does not display itself haughtily. It is not conceited—arrogant and inflated with pride; it is not rude (unmannerly), and does not act unbecomingly.

"Love [God's love in us] does not insist on its own rights or its own way, for it is not self-seeking; it is not touchy or fretful or resentful; it takes no account of the evil done to it—pays no attention to a suffered wrong. It does not rejoice at injustice and unrighteousness, but rejoices when right and truth prevail.

"Love bears up under anything and everything that comes, is ever ready to believe the best of every person, its hopes are fadeless under all circumstances and it endures everything [without weakening]."

Remember, you do not have the power to love like that, but Jesus Christ can love through you, if you allow Him to.

Giving Your Expectations to God

The basis for your discontentment and inability to accept your husband lies in your expectations of him and his failure to meet your goals. When he fails to live up to your expectations, you may be hurt, irritated, and disappointed. You and your husband will only be contented and free when you quit setting goals and stop expecting him to be who he is not.

Mary was a virtual prisoner of her own preconceived ideas of how her husband should act. She was raised in a home where proper table manners were expected. When her husband Don first came to the table in his undershirt and then put his elbows on the table, she was shocked. As time went on, she found that he had other habits she considered uncouth. She tried to correct him, but instead of changing Don, her efforts only put a strain on their relationship.

When Mary finally committed her expectations to God, the tension between her and Don disappeared. After that when her husband came to the table properly dressed, she was grateful. When his manners didn't come up to her expectations, she wasn't disappointed. In the climate of her acceptance, Don began to choose better etiquette himself.

If, like Mary, you are disappointed in your husband, you may be trying to make him meet the need in your life that only Christ can meet. "He who believes in Him [Christ]— who adheres to, trusts in and relies on Him—shall never be disappointed or put to shame" (1 Peter 2:6). Let your disappointment be a signal to worship only Christ.

Changing Your Husband

It may seem only right to help your husband change attitudes, traits, and actions that are making him unhappy. But your well-meaning efforts will communicate to him, "I don't love you as you are. I want you to be different." A man wants his wife to be proud, not ashamed of him. When she is not, he becomes discouraged. The masculine abilities God has given him to cope with life are crushed instead of liberated. He cannot live a healthy, satisfying life when constantly on trial. Your intentions may be sincere but can lead to disaster. God says, "There is a way that seemeth right unto a man, but the end thereof are the ways of death" (Proverbs 16:25, KJV).

God did not give you the job of convicting your husband of sin or error. That is the work of the Holy Spirit (see John 16:8-11). When you take on that job, you only get in God's way and slow down His work. Neither are you to be your husband's mother—correcting and training him. Having good intentions for his future is not enough. You must act upon the principles set forth in God's Word.

Communication breaks down in an atmosphere of nonacceptance. When your husband tells you what he has said or done, don't criticize, point out where he was wrong, or tell him what he should have done. If you do, he may decide it is less painful to keep his thoughts to himself and stop confiding in you. Only when he is sure of your total acceptance will he confide in you. If you hold his confidences sacred, he'll know he can trust you not to ridicule or belittle him. If you must tell his secrets to someone, tell them to Jesus Christ.

You, the Critic

Are you aware that unasked-for advice is really veiled criticism? Yes, giving unasked-for advice is just another way of attempting to change your man. A friend of mine, Tammy, had stopped her obvious methods of correcting her husband Jack. Yet Jack was not confiding in her freely, and Tammy could not understand why.

One day as they were driving along, he started telling her about one of his business transactions. Tammy began to respond in her usual way with "I would have done so and so" and "Why didn't you handle it this way?"

Jack suddenly stopped talking. When she finally got him to tell her what was wrong, he said, "You never approve or agree with anything I do. I shouldn't have tried to share this with you."

Tammy had not realized that her unasked-for advice was actually criticism of him. She honestly had not intended to put him down. Sadly, she realized that her advice or veiled criticism told Jack that she did not accept him as he was.

Let's see what Jesus had to say about criticism. "Don't criticize and then you won't be criticized! For others will treat you as you treat them. And why worry about a speck in the eye of a brother when you have a board in your own? Should you say, 'Friend, let me help you get that speck out of your eye,' when you can't even see because of the board in your own? Hypocrite! First get rid of the board. Then you can see to help your brother" (Matthew 7:1-5, LB).

When you criticize your husband or anyone else, you are assuming an "I'm better than you are," attitude. Wouldn't it be wiser to ask God to show you your failures and let Him deal with your husband as He sees best? Make it a habit, when you have the desire to change something about your husband, to ask Christ to show you your own faults. If you follow Jesus' advice to "be humble, thinking of others as better than yourself" (Philippians 2:3, LB), your critical, self-righteous, or martyr attitude will disappear.

Don't try to change your husband by demanding your own way. Though you may feel you have succeeded in some area when he gives in, he may just want to keep peace in the household. Over a period of time, your domineering attitude may develop a coolness in your man and eventually destroy his love for you. You may win a few battles, but you will lose the war. Forfeiting a beautiful, fulfilling marital relationship is not worth the temporary "success."

Your Neighbor's Model Husband

Trying to change your husband by using other men as shining examples does not work either. Refrain from pointing out the neighbor who keeps his yard well-manicured when you want your husband to work in yours. If you remind him of the expensive wardrobe Bill bought Jane, or about your dad's success in handling a situation, you are shouting loud and clear, "I am not pleased with you as you are." Manipulation won't encourage your husband to love and cherish you.

When you do not accept your husband the way he is, he may rebel, as the writer of Proverbs suggests. "The north wind brings forth rain; so does a backbiting tongue [of a wife] bring forth an angry countenance [in her husband]. It is better to dwell in the corner of the housetop than to share a house with a disagreeing, quarrelsome, and scolding woman" (Proverbs 25:23-24). Naturally, a man rebels. He is struggling to maintain his freedom to become the man God meant him to be.

You may not feel that your actions classify you as disagreeable, quarrelsome, or scolding though your husband has been acting angry and rebellious. Ask God to show you how you may unknowingly be the cause of his bad temper. If Christ does point out some wrong thing in your behavior, confess it as sin and trust Him to live through you and change you. Realize that He can cause your mistakes to work together for your good as you turn to Him for guidance. God promises His chil-

dren, "I will restore or replace for you the years that the locust
has eaten. . . . And my people shall never be put to shame"
(Joel 2:25-26).

God's Formula for Accepting Your Husband

God has a plan through which you can learn to accept your
husband. It is clearly outlined in Philippians 4:4, 6-8 (BECK):
"Be happy in the Lord always! . . . Don't worry about anything, but in everything go to God, and pray to let Him know
what you want, and give thanks. Then God's peace, better
than our thinking, will guard your hearts and minds in Christ
Jesus. . . . Keep your minds on all that is true or noble, right or
pure, lovely or appealing, on anything that is excellent or that
deserves praise."

The first step in God's plan is to commit all of your problems to Him. Regardless of what has worried, upset, or irritated you, Christ says you should tell Him about it. Then let
Him work it out. Resist the impulse to return to the problem
because you've "thought of something else that might work."
Trust Him for the solution. If you don't, you're saying in effect, "God, You are not able to handle my problem."

Don't be like the man who was walking along the road with
a heavy load on his back. A farmer stopped to give him a ride.
The man climbed onto the farmer's truck but left the load on
his back. "Why don't you put your load down on the truck?"
the farmer called out to him.

"It was so kind of you to give me a ride," the man answered, "I don't want to ask you to carry my load too."

How foolish! But that is what you do when you do not let
Jesus Christ carry all of your burdens. He died for you and
paid for your sins. He offers you victory over each problem
and is pleased when you claim it (see 1 Corinthians 10:13).

How do you commit your burdens or problems to God? By
talking to Him about them. That's prayer—simply opening

up to God, knowing He understands perfectly. God will not force His solutions on you even though He is God of the universe. Instead, He waits for you to come to Him and share with Him and ask for His help.

Since He sees things from a different viewpoint and knows what's best for you, don't limit Him by telling Him when and how to answer your prayers. Let Him work out your problems according to His timing and plan. Then thank Him for answering, trusting Him to do what is best.

After giving your problems to God and thanking Him for taking care of them, fix your mind on whatever pure, honorable, and praiseworthy qualities your husband has (if your problem involves him). Does he get up each morning, regardless of how he feels, and go to work? Thank God. Is he kind and gentle to the children? Thank the Lord. Is he a sociable guy? Be grateful.

If you have a hard time thinking of some positive traits, think back to the qualities that drew you to him before marriage. Those traits are still in him but may have been buried during the years of your marriage. Concentrate on his positive traits and his weaknesses will diminish. This idea is different from a "self-improvement" plan because you're trusting God to improve you and your husband as you follow His formula.

It might be comforting to realize that negative traits are distorted positive traits. If negative traits can be modified or channeled in the right direction, they can become strengths. Stubbornness can become perseverance. Cowardice can be turned to gentleness. Tactlessness can be turned to frankness. If you trust Jesus Christ to take care of your husband's problems, and fix your mind on his assets, you can help him turn bad traits into good ones.

The results you can expect are described in Philippians 4:8. You will experience God's peace which is more wonderful than the human mind can understand. It is a deep, inner quietness that depends not on circumstances, but on your relationship with Jesus Christ.

The formula can be stated in this way: Problems transferred to Christ, plus focusing on the positive, equals peace.

Application

Now that you know you should accept your husband as he is, try to apply the principle in your own marriage relationship. Look for opportunities to tell your husband that you are glad he is the kind of man he is. Tell him you know that you have made many mistakes and are willing to correct them. Explain that you realize you have not been the loving, understanding, submissive wife you should have been. Show your husband through your actions as well as your words that you accept him as he is. Both of you will begin to experience the sheer joy and freedom that comes from following God's principles.

4
Helping Your Husband Love Himself

The key to fulfillment and contentment in your life is described by Jesus: " 'You must love the Lord your God with your whole heart, your whole soul, and your whole mind.' This is the greatest command, and is first in importance. The second is like it: 'You must love your neighbor as you do yourself' " (Matthew 22:37-39, WMS). When the first commandment is true in your life, the second can become a reality. Furthermore, you cannot love someone else until you first love yourself. And you can love yourself only when you see yourself from God's viewpoint. In the Bible you will discover:

1. You are a person of *worth* and *value*—so valuable, that Jesus Christ was willing to leave the glories of heaven, become the God-Man, live a sinless life, and die to pay for your sins. If you were the only person to ever live, He still would have died for only you (see 1 Peter 1: 18-22).

2. You *belong* to the Royal Family and have the greatest heritage possible. As a member of God's family, you need never feel inferior.

3. If you're a Christian, God accepts you as you are.
4. He loves you unconditionally.
5. If you're a Christian, God promises to provide all of your needs. "My God will amply supply your every need, through Christ Jesus, from His riches in glory" (Philippians 4:19, WMS). When you realize who you are in Christ, you can be free of feelings of guilt or inferiority and begin to love yourself. Once you love yourself, you can genuinely love your husband and meet the needs of his life that God has meant you to meet.

One of those needs is described in Ephesians 5:33: "Let the wife see that she respects and reverences her husband—that she notices him, regards him, honors him, prefers him, venerates and esteems him; and that she defers to him, praises him, and loves and admires him exceedingly." Your man has a strong need to know you are proud of him, pleased with him, and admire him.

Nothing will be too big for him if he has your loving support and admiration. You see, a compliment acts as a stimulus and is a source of encouragement; whereas, a complaint acts as a depressant and is a source of discouragement.

As you fulfill your husband's need for admiration, you will help him love himself. He, in turn, then will be able to nourish, protect, and cherish you as described in Ephesians 5:28-29: "Even so husbands should love their wives as [being in a sense] their own bodies. He who loves his own wife loves himself. For no man ever hated his own flesh, but nourishes and carefully protects and cherishes it, as Christ does the Church."

Knowing that God made you and your husband different so you would complement each other should give you an incentive to meet his need for praise and admiration. Remember, each of you is unfulfilled alone, but together, you make a whole. Your husband's need for admiration is fulfilled through your genuine praise. His love and strength in turn should meet your need for tenderness and protection. Your intuition complements his wisdom. Your loyal support undergirds his initiative. When you and your husband use these abilities to strengthen each other, you will develop a lasting marriage.

You'll find further motivation in understanding your role in marriage as described in 1 Corinthians 11:7, KJV: "For a man . . . is the image and glory of God; but the woman is the glory of the man." As man allows Jesus Christ to control his life by the power of the Holy Spirit, Christ's qualities are manifested through him and he reflects God's glory. His wife, however, is to reflect her husband's glory. She does this by bringing attention to his commendable qualities, by praising him, honoring him, and giving him proper distinction.

As you sincerely praise your husband, you may need help in uncovering traits, interests, or strengths that you can honestly admire. Discovering things about him that you may have overlooked for years will be exciting. How do you go about detecting these hidden qualities?

1. Watch your husband
If you want a manly man, praise him for his physical strength and the ease with which he does manly or difficult things such as opening tight jars, moving furniture, mowing the lawn, and handling heavy equipment rather than praising him for doing easier tasks usually thought of as women's work, such as dishes and dusting. Express appreciation whenever he does any of the usual chores around the house instead of saying, "Well, it's about time."

Your appreciation and gratitude should gradually encourage him to do things around the house if he has been unwilling to do them before. But don't be discouraged if his first reaction to "Wow, you sure have strong arms!" is "Yours would be strong, too, if you ever used them." He may have built a wall around himself because he's missed your appreciation in the past. Give him time.

Compliment him on his broad shoulders, deep voice, strong hands, and yes, even on his beard—though you may feel like saying, "I wish you'd shave that thing off!"

Praise or show appreciation for his courage, honor, determination, cleverness, intellectual ability, achievements, skills, leadership, aspirations, and/or ideals. Have you thanked him lately for the many hours he spends earning a living for your family? His faithfulness in providing for you demonstrates praiseworthy qualities of dependability and responsibility.

Praise him for the way in which he stands behind his convictions as he directs your home and household. You may not always agree with his decisions, but you can compliment him for his courage in standing by them. Approve and compliment his determination when he accomplishes his goals. You may have been calling his determination stubbornness. If you see it as a worthy trait, God can use you to turn it to His use. (Be sure to ask God to show you ways you can apply this principle of admiration.)

These are just a few suggestions to get you started. Now a word of caution: Start off gently, trusting Christ to point out things in your husband you can sincerely praise. If you come on too strong at first, you may appear phony.

If you have a son, be sure to praise him for masculine qualities and traits too. Your wisely given encouragement will help him develop into a stronger man, one with a better understanding of himself and God's role for him.

Be sure that your motives are right when you praise your men. If you do it so you can change or manipulate them, they'll think you're flattering them or "buttering them up." Ask God to give you pure motives and then, in faith, believe He will.

2. Listen to him

Even if your husband is talking about something you don't understand or feel interested in, give him your undivided attention. You'll learn a lot about him. You will begin to detect how he feels about people and situations. You will even discover noble, mature dimensions in his character that you never knew were there.

Many of us wives don't know our husbands because we never quit talking long enough to listen to them. Scripture says, "Let a woman learn in quietness in entire submissiveness" (1 Timothy 2:11).

3. Develop an interest in things he likes

If you are married to a sportsman, learn enough about his favorite sports so he can talk to you about them. But don't become an expert. He will enjoy teaching you some things himself if you show an interest. You may not believe it now, but after you learn something about his interests, whether they be sports or hobbies, you will most likely find that you enjoy them too.

Don't Get Discouraged

At first you may feel utterly foolish praising your husband. But if you remind yourself of his need, and continue by faith, you will find that words of praise come more and more easily. As a matter of fact, you will probably find that you like to give praise as much as he enjoys receiving it.

Many women feel that their husbands are already too egocentric and are afraid that if they openly express admiration, their husbands will become more boastful. Actually, the opposite will probably occur. The man who constantly brags about himself usually feels insecure and is trying to convince himself and you that he's great.

"Showing off" is his attempt to bolster his ego. Give him

your attention and praise, and soon he will begin to believe in himself and no longer feel the need to boast. Should he be truly egocentric, your job is not to correct his weakness, but to support and encourage him. As you pray for him, trust God to deal with his problem.

After applying these principles of admiration, Carol said excitedly, "I can't get over how my husband is 'eating this up!' Yesterday he stayed home for lunch about an hour and a half instead of his usual 30 minutes. I thought he would never go back to work." Laughingly, she continued, "If he keeps this up, I'll never get any work done." Of course, she was enjoying his attentiveness as much as he was relishing her admiration.

As you trust Jesus Christ to help you understand your husband, you will be pleasantly surprised to discover what a wonderful man you married. For the first time, you may see that he has been expressing his love for you all along. Because he did not always show it in a tender, sensitive way, you hadn't recognized it as love.

Perhaps he straightened up the kitchen after an argument, or teases you constantly, or made you that special cabinet you've wanted, or even dug up the ground by the garage so you could plant roses. Don't force your husband to express his love the way you do. Accept these loving gestures, even his constant teasing, as his way of saying he loves you.

If you have a hard time finding admirable qualities in your man, believe, by faith, that they do exist although they may be dormant. "Love bears up under anything and everything that comes, is ever ready to believe the best of every person, its hopes are fadeless under all circumstances and it endures everything [without weakening]" (1 Corinthians 13:7). Your unwavering belief in him will begin to reveal his positive traits. Don't push him—just believe in him, and you will begin to experience a deeper, closer relationship with your man.

Your Reward

Do you feel this marriage relationship is all one-sided, that your husband receives all the benefits? Well, cheer up. When you follow God's plan for your life, you will be rewarded threefold. First, as your husband begins to respond to your loving admiration, one of your rewards will be his own expression of appreciation and love for you. God's Word teaches, "For whatsoever a man soweth, that shall he also reap" (Galatians 6:7, KJV). Your loving patience and kindness to your husband will encourage the highest and best in him. That is worth working toward.

Every man is different, of course. One will quickly and lovingly react to his wife's overtures. Another will neither react quickly nor easily. It is your job to patiently respond to God and your husband in loving submission. It is God's place to work in your husband's life. Trust God to repair any damage done to your marriage relationship because you have not let Jesus Christ control your life. If you have sown seeds of bitterness, jealousy, or selfishness for years, it may take some time for God to get rid of the weeds.

However, do try to be honest and objective. Do not assume responsibilities that are your husband's alone. Realize that there are needs in his life that you cannot meet, such as his need to make Christ Lord in his life or his need for acceptance and approval by others in business and society. Your main job is to comfort, encourage, and support your man when he is with you.

Second, Jesus Christ will give you inner peace and stability when you live to please and obey Him and not yourself (see Romans 8:6-7). If you accept your husband as he is, admire him, and care for your household because Christ instructs you to, you will not be "puffed up" when your husband praises you for your efforts. Nor will you be discouraged when he fails to praise you for a job well done. You will realize that what follows as a result of your obedience to Christ is His responsibility. "I am convinced and sure of this very thing, that He who began a good work in you will continue until the day of Jesus Christ—right up to the time of His return—developing [that good work] and perfecting and bringing it to full completion in you" (Philippians 1:6).

If, for instance, you cleaned your house just to receive your husband's praise, only to have him say, "Hey, you missed that cobweb in the corner," your day would be spoiled. But if you cleaned the house first of all to please the Lord, you would not be so hurt.

Third, you will receive rewards in eternity as you trust and obey Christ for every need. "Whatever you do, do your work heartily, as for the Lord rather than for men; knowing that from the Lord you will receive the reward of your inheritance. It is the Lord Christ whom you serve" (Colossians 3:23-24, NASB).

When you are tempted to "throw in the towel," remember that if you faithfully trust Christ, you will receive both earthly and eternal rewards. "If any man's work . . . remains, he shall receive a reward" (1 Corinthians 3:14, NASB).

It took this very principle of eternal rewards to jolt me into confessing a sin in my life one day. I was very angry with a certain individual and was verbally tearing her apart—and enjoying it. I knew I was wrong and could expect discipline from Christ if I didn't confess my sin (see Hebrews 12:6). But my attitude was, "I have a few more things I want to say first."

After some time, God brought the principle of eternal rewards to my mind, reminding me that my sinful attitude would cause misery for me now and I would lose my eternal rewards (see 1 Corinthians 3:11-15). That's all the reminder I needed to help me realize that I did not want to pay the high price of sin.

You will not regret trusting Jesus Christ. Under His plan, you can expect maximum benefits, both for you and for your husband.

5

Not Second Best

In order to fulfill your role as a wife adequately, you must understand the place God expects your husband to occupy in your life. When we examine Ephesians 5:24, we see that the husband-wife relationship parallels Christ's relationship with the Church (all believers). "As the Church is subject to Christ, so let wives also be subject in everything to their husbands." You, as a believer, are to depend totally on Jesus Christ for your very existence. When Jesus is first in your inner spiritual life, He will enable you to put your husband first in your human relationships and activities.

When your husband has the assurance that he is first in your life, his self-confidence will be strengthened; he will be more able to face the world. The fact that he may have been cut down by his business opponents will be less painful if he can return to the haven of his home where you accept, admire, and support him.

However, remember that it is your support, not your protection that your husband needs. He will develop traits of independence, courage, and confidence only as he faces and tackles his problems—with your support, not your protection or smothering. If you're tempted to feel sorry for him, remember that most men thrive on the challenge of caring for and protecting their families, not on being cared for and protected.

At the time of marriage, you and your husband became one or "one flesh" (see Genesis 2:24). Now, no normal person will ever intentionally harm himself. Yet wives often unintentionally hurt their husbands—their own flesh. As you give Jesus Christ more and more freedom to control you, He will enable you to begin to love your husband as you love yourself and you will not want to hurt him in any way.

As you search God's Word, as you study the principles we're discussing, and as you allow Christ to control your life, He will enable you to love your husband as yourself. He'll show you ways in which you may be hurting your man. Trust God to help you correct any harmful attitudes. Then you will become the blessing to your husband that God describes in Proverbs 18:22 (LB): "The man who finds a wife finds a good thing; she is a blessing to him from the Lord." What a privilege we have to be able to meet our husbands' needs!

Attitudes and Actions to Avoid

Disloyalty: As you study your Bible, you will discover that certain attitudes and actions are not in harmony with God's plan for you as a responder. *Disloyalty* to your man is one. If you love your husband as yourself, you will protect him and be loyal to him in his presence or absence. "[Love] doesn't plan to hurt anyone. It doesn't delight in evil but is happy with the truth. It bears everything, believes everything, hopes for everything, endures everything. Love never dies" (1 Corinthians 13:5-7, BECK).

Being loyal means that you will confess as sin and give up any critical attitude you may have toward your husband. Trust Jesus Christ to show you good, positive things to say about him, rather than negative things. Your criticism of or uncomplimentary attitude toward your husband, especially in front of others, can hurt him as much as a slap in the face.

Even criticism directed toward someone other than your husband may cost you his respect and trust. He will think, and no doubt justly, that your critical attitude does not stop with certain people but influences all your relationships.

It may help you to realize that the very faults that irritate you in others are usually the ones you have trouble with yourself. That is why they irritate you. Christ said, "Don't judge, so that you will not be judged. . . . Why do you look at the speck in your brother's eye and don't notice the log in your own eye?" (Matthew 7:1, 3, BECK)

"Therefore you have no excuse or defense or justification, O man, whoever you are who judges and condemns another. For in posing as judge and passing sentence on another you condemn yourself, because you who judge are habitually practicing the very same things [that you censure and denounce]" (Romans 2:1).

Selfishness: Be sure you aren't giving your husband the feeling that he rates last. After spending hours washing, cleaning, and cooking for him, you may think you are the epitome of unselfishness. But whose desires do you consider when you accept or reject a dinner engagement? Whose likes and dislikes do you consider when planning a meal? Whose errands do you run first? When you buy your husband something to wear, do you buy what you want or what you know he likes best?

Do you plan your activities so you can stop and visit with him if he should need to talk when he gets home from work? Remember, he can easily tell if he does not have your complete attention when he talks to you. The uninterested look on your face, glancing at the clock or out of the window, or yawning will give you away. Your interest must be sincere.

Jealousy: You'll also have to beware of jealousy if you are to love your husband as yourself. Jealousy tells your husband that you love yourself more than you love him because you want what makes *you* happy rather than what makes *him* happy. Jealousy is simply denying another person pleasures that may draw him away from you. You may resent his "night out with the boys," his time-consuming career, or some other activity or person. Yet if you love him as you love yourself, you will give him liberty to have any pleasure that makes him happy.

"What if I lose him?" you may ask. That's a normal concern. But do remember that you belong to Jesus Christ. Trust Him with your fears, and He will protect your interests. "Then you will lie down in peace and safety, unafraid; and I will bind you to Me forever with chains of righteousness and justice and love and mercy. I will betroth you to Me in faithfulness, and love, and you will really know Me then as you never have before" (Hosea 2:18-20, LB). If you ask God to take away your jealousy, and trust Him to help you win rather than lose your husband's love.

However, if you continue to check up on your husband, you can expect strained relations with him. "Jealousy makes [the wronged] man furious; therefore, he will not spare in the day of vengeance [upon the detected ones]" (Proverbs 6:34).

The secret of healthy lives for both husband and wife is found in Proverbs 14:30: "A calm and undisturbed mind and heart are the life and health of the body, but envy, jealousy, and wrath are as rottenness of the bones."

After hearing these principles about jealousy, Sarah realized that her jealousy was one of the main factors in causing her husband to leave her and ask for a divorce. Right away she set about getting her relationship with the Lord straightened out by confessing to Him, as sin, her jealousy, bitterness, resentfulness, and desire for revenge. Even though her husband had been stepping out on her, she committed the situation to the Lord, trusting Him to look after her interests.

As she trusted God, moment by moment, her life began to take on a new stability, expressed in a calm and gentle spirit. During the rare occasions when her husband was home, she began to show him that she accepted him as he was. She admired him instead of criticizing him and gave him the freedom to do what he wanted to do and to be the man he wanted to be. In other words, she made the time they spent together enjoyable for both of them.

Within a few weeks he moved back home. As time went on, he began staying home all day on his day off—quite a victory. Then one day as they sat by their backyard pool talking, he commented, "It is just great spending time with you."

Bossiness: Finally, don't tell your husband how to run his life. When he shares his problems with you, avoid responding to him as you like him to respond to you. Generally, when we women have problems, we want solutions from our men. We are comforted when they either remove or solve our problems. (By the way, do not ask your husband for help with a problem unless you are ready to accept his advice or solution.)

On the other hand, when your man has a problem, he doesn't need your solutions. He needs you to listen, to be sympathetic, and to restore his self-esteem by encouraging him to make his own decision. In other words, you need to reinforce his faith in himself so he will be free to use his God-given, masculine ability to conquer the situation.

Areas of Potential Imbalance

When you center your activities around your husband, you will have a happy man and a balanced life yourself. In other words, you will be the satisfied, complete woman you want to be. As you give your man his right place, you will find him more willing to give you freedom to enjoy other interests and activities as long as they don't become a threat to his role or position. Many men act possessive and domineering because they feel that their masculine role or position in their wives' affections is insecure.

This diagram explains the proper balance:

When the husband is at the hub of your activities, and the spokes (other elements) of your life are in correct proportion, the wheel (your life) will roll smoothly. If the spokes get out of adjustment, the wheel will wobble or even crash in its course. It is imbalance of the spokes that causes the problem, not necessarily any spoke or activity itself.

1. Homemaking

While a good thing in itself, homemaking can easily get out of balance and dominate your life. A woman who likes to keep an immaculate house may insist that her husband remove his shoes before walking on her freshly polished floors. Or she may not allow him to sit on the sofa because he will mess up the cushions. Her home, rather than her husband, is first in her life.

On the other hand, some women's homes look as if a cyclone had struck—total confusion and disorder. This is not honoring to Jesus Christ either. We are told in 1 Corinthians 14:33 that God is not a God of confusion and disorder but of peace and order. In other words, there must be a balance. A man's home should be his haven, a place where he can relax and be himself. It should be a source of enjoyment and peace for him.

2. Children

Children are meant to be a blessing to you. "Children are a gift from God; they are His reward. Children born to a young man are like sharp arrows to defend him. Happy is the man who has his quiver full of them. That man shall have the help he needs when arguing with his enemies" (Psalm 127:3-5, LB).

If you put your children first, however, your children will not be the joy God meant them to be to you and your husband. It is so easy to center your life around them and their activities and needs and neglect your husband. You tend to think, "Well, he is an adult and can look after himself. My children are young and need me so desperately." Remember, God made woman because man needed her. The relationship between you and your husband is meant to continue until death. Your children will be with you only a short time.

Not that you should neglect your children. When your priorities are in order, you will find you have adequate time for both. The family will be a closer unit. Your children will feel secure with parents who love each other, and your husband won't be likely to resent the children for taking his place in your life. You give your best to your children when your husband is the hub of your life.

3. Appearance
Your appearance is another area that communicates to your husband his importance in your life. Remember, he may be exposed to stimulating, well-groomed women in the business world, and they remind him of his need for a woman. He rushes home to be with his wife, eagerly opens the door—and there you are!

His anticipations are either fulfilled or disappointed. Even though you may have four preschoolers and mountains of diapers and dishes to manage, you should arrange, whenever possible, to spend a few minutes before his arrival freshening up. Your husband does not want to be taken for granted any more than you do. So be sure you don't spend all your time shopping, grooming, and sewing to look nice for others rather than for him. Give him your best and you will reap the dividends.

Of course you can overdo in the area of grooming, spending so much time and money on yourself and your own looks that your husband may wonder if you are dressing to please him or attract other men. Grooming can become a very self-centered activity. Like other areas of your life, this one needs to be balanced.

4. Money and Security
It is very easy for the area or "spoke" of money and security

to dominate your life. Poor handling of money or the lack of money can be a constant source of friction between you and your husband.

Books have been written on the subject of money management so we won't discuss the subject here except to point out that you and your husband should plan the handling of your income early in your marriage. Here again, you may offer advice but your husband should manage the money and keep the books unless he specifically asks you to do this job for him.

Interestingly, the Bible speaks about a happy man being able to trust his wife in buying and selling, so it is quite biblical for a man to commit his household and money matters into his wife's hands if she is wise in those matters. "Her husband can trust her, and she will richly satisfy his needs. She goes out to inspect a field, and buys it; with her own hands she plants a vineyard. She makes belted linen garments to sell to the merchants" (Proverbs 31:11, 16, 24, LB).

When money is in short supply, your attitude toward the situation and your husband's struggle to bring in enough can either make or break him. Possibly more than at any other time, your husband needs your support and encouragement then. Men feel as if they've failed if they can't supply the family income. Without proper support from their wives, men have turned to alcohol, other women, and even suicide during times of financial crisis. If you scold, nag, or fret, you will only increase your husband's sense of failure.

Beware that the need for security doesn't kill your husband's incentive at work. You may resist his taking a promotion. You don't want to move, or you feel that your way of life will be threatened. If you take that attitude, you may see your husband's interest in you and his work and life itself begin to wane.

Put your trust in God, rather than your situation and finances, and you'll be able to face changes in your husband's career gracefully. God warns against trying to gain security from possessions. "He who leans on, trusts and is confident in his riches shall fall, but the [uncompromisingly] righteous shall flourish like a green bough" (Proverbs 11:28). A man can be a greater success financially if he is not distracted by an unfulfilled wife but has her support and encouragement.

5. In-laws

Another area that can be turned from a blessing to a curse when out of balance is the relationship of you and your husband to your parents. The Lord made provision for the in-law problem before it was a reality. He told Adam and Eve, "A man shall leave his father and mother and shall become united and cleave to his wife, and they shall become one flesh" (Genesis 2:24).

Once you and your husband become one flesh in marriage, your husband, not your parents, is to be the center of your life. Of course, you are to continue to honor and respect your parents and his. Call or write them occasionally and share some bit of family news: a child's good report card, some cute thing a young child has said or done, your husband's promotion. "Honor (esteem and value as precious) your father and your mother; this is the first commandment with a promise: that all may be well with you and that you may live long on the earth" (Ephesians 6:2-3). You can benefit from their maturity and experience as they give you words of counsel.

However, problems arise when you honor your parents' wishes and desires above your husband's. Do not make your husband feel that he must compete with your parents—or with his. When he knows he is first in your life, he will appreciate the parents who gave him such a wonderful wife.

6. Outside activities

The last "spoke" we'll discuss is that of outside activities: social life, church work, clubs, and so forth. "Surely my husband knows he is more important than my outside interests," you may say. How is he to know it? He must judge by what he sees and hears. If you spend most of your time directing the women's missionary group at church or a Girl Scout troop, what conclusion can he reach other than that those activities are more important to you than he is?

Even though activities are good in themselves they can take so much of your time and attention that your husband feels he is less important to you than they are. As a matter of fact, if you talk too much about Jesus Christ or are habitually reading your Bible in front of him or are always going to Gospel meetings, your husband could begin to feel about Christ the same way he would feel about a man with whom you were having an affair. This may sound ridiculous, but perhaps all he knows is that someone besides himself has priority in your life.

A non-Christian does not grasp spiritual truths. "But the man who isn't a Christian can't understand and can't accept these thoughts from God which the Holy Spirit teaches us. They sound foolish to him, because only those who have the Holy Spirit within them can understand what the Holy Spirit means. Others just can't take it in" (1 Corinthians 2:14, LB). A Christian husband can also be "turned off" to spiritual truth by an overenthusiastic Christian wife who is constantly talking about spiritual truths she has just discovered.

You win your husband to spiritual values by incorporating them into your life, thereby becoming the wife he wants you to be. "In like manner, you married women, be submissive to your own husbands—subordinate yourselves as being secondary to and dependent on them, and adapt yourselves to them. So that even if any do not obey the Word [of God], they may be won over not by discussion but by the [godly] lives of their wives, when they observe the pure and modest way in which you conduct yourselves, together with your reverence" (1

Peter 3:1-2). This does not mean living by some group's "do's or don'ts," however.

Suppose you and your husband are enjoying certain activities together when suddenly you become a Christian and start changing your way of life. He finds himself spending time alone because you are either at church or refuse to go certain places with him that you once enjoyed together. Your husband may feel threatened by the sudden changes in you because he sees your relationship being destroyed.

I am sure you have heard that the Word of God divides people. "Do not think that I have come to bring peace upon the earth; I have not come to bring peace but a sword. For I have come to part asunder a man from his father, and a daughter from her mother, and a newly married wife from her mother-in-law; and a man's foes will be they of his own household" (Matthew 10:34-36). Notice that every family relationship is mentioned here *except the marital relationship.* Might this omission not be significant? The fact that the marital relationship is not mentioned suggests that God does not divide a married couple. He does not divide what He has united into one flesh. Rather, His Word properly applied will produce a precious marriage relationship.

You may say, "Then why the verses in 1 Corinthians 7:13-16 about letting an unsaved husband leave you if he chooses?" God gives these directions so that a Christian can peacefully deal with any marital problems that may arise. Division in the home comes from sin in the life of husband or wife, not from God.

Usually, as a woman trusts Jesus Christ, her life will demonstrate a stability and inner happiness that will help draw her husband to Christ. But not always. "For how do you know, O wife, whether you will save your husband? Or how do you know, O husband, whether you will save your wife?" (1 Corinthians 7:16, NASB)

Regardless of the spiritual status of your husband, however, your role, your way of relating to him should be the same. If he is a Christian, or when he becomes one, you will share spiritual truths together as he takes the lead or initiates the conversation. Generally speaking, the spiritual truths you learn are for your own edification, not for you to teach to your husband. When you have the strong desire to share these things, pray for your husband instead.

Margaret applied these principles. When James asked how she had become such a wonderful wife, she gently explained, "Jesus Christ is the source of my inner peace; He gives me the power to be the wife I should be." In responding to her husband as she did, Margaret did not make him feel that she no longer needed him. Christ had enabled her to willingly be dependent on her husband.

When a man is the center of his wife's life, he will rarely seek out another woman. Sex is seldom the primary reason for a man's promiscuity. He is usually looking for a woman who will accept him as he is, admire him, need him, and give him first place in her life.

Reconstruction Program

Do you feel that making your husband the true center of your life is too big an order for you to fill? I hope so, because then you will see your need to let Jesus Christ take over and do it for you. Your order is not too big for Him to fill. He is the only One who can make you the real woman you want to be. "A wise, understanding and prudent wife is from the Lord" (Proverbs 19:14).

Jesus Christ can use the laboratory of marriage to make you a godly woman. "A capable, intelligent, and virtuous woman, who is he who can find her? She is far more precious than jewels, and her value is far above rubies or pearls" (Proverbs 31:10). I think it is significant that a pearl is mentioned here.

A pearl is formed under water through suffering. Frequently God uses difficult circumstances, even marriage problems, to make you His pearl.

Marriage reveals the real you. It brings out your habit patterns and exposes you for what you really are. Your husband does not make you what you are; he simply acts as a stimulus to bring out what is on the inside. "Keep your heart with all vigilance and above all that you guard, for out of it flow the springs of life" (Proverbs 4:23).

True, you will always have the Old Sin Nature (OSN) until Christ takes you to be with Him, but you do not have to be under its control. If Jesus Christ is the source of power in your life, He will enable you to form new response patterns to life situations. You will not need to be a slave to the Old Sin Nature. He will enable you to break the hold of the OSN and its habit patterns (see Romans 8:1-4). Each time you feel the pull of the OSN, as it tries to control you, simply turn to God and ask for His deliverance from the temptation to respond in the old sinful pattern.

Do understand that temptation itself or an evil thought in itself is not sin. It is what you do with that thought or temptation that determines whether or not it becomes sin. "But every person is tempted when he is drawn away, enticed and baited by his own desire (lust, passions). Then, his own evil desire when it has conceived gives birth to sin, and sin when it is fully matured brings forth death" (James 1:14-15).

The following diagram of a phonograph shows the choice we have. We may play the record of old habit patterns formed by the OSN. Or we may push the reject button on the old record and drop into place the new record of life in the Spirit.

The choice is yours. You will discover that as you trust Christ to control you, all areas of your life will begin to fall into line with God's plan for you. When Christ is first in your inner spiritual life, He will direct you to put your husband

NEW HABIT PATTERNS

YOUR CHOICE

OLD
HABIT
PATTERNS

REJECT CONTROL
KNOB (1 JOHN 1:9)

first in your human relationships and activities because this is
His plan for you as a wife.

6

Follow the Leader

Someone must assume major responsibilities, make decisions and direct activities in any functioning unit to prevent dis·order and chaos. Any successful business or organization rec·ognizes this need. Yet frequently families ignore the principle of leadership and therefore do not experience the harmony and peace God meant them to enjoy. Since the family is the basic unit of society, its stability will determine not only the security and happiness of its members but also the strength of the nation. Stability for both home and nation depends on recognizing the man as head of the family.

The Divine Order
God designated the man as the undisputed head of the family when He said to Eve, "Your desire and craving shall be for your husband, and he shall rule over you" (Genesis 3:16). This same principle is reaffirmed in the New Testament in Ephesians 5:22-23 (LB): "You wives must submit to your husbands' leadership in the same way you submit to the Lord. For a husband is in charge of his wife in the same way Christ

is in charge of His body the Church. (He gave His very life to take care of it and be its Saviour!) So you wives must willingly obey your husbands in everything, just as the Church obeys Christ." *Society* did not assign the position of leadership to man; he was *divinely* appointed "head of the family."

A home with two heads or with the wife as the head could be called a monstrosity because the order of the man's and woman's roles has been distorted, thereby creating an abnormal condition. As homes have become more wife-dominated, there has been a rise in juvenile delinquency, rebellion, homosexuality, the divorce rate, and the number of frustrated women, because the home was designed by God to run efficiently with the man as the leader. Ignoring this principle of his leadership or devising substitutes creates untold problems.

God's order for the home is that the husband be the head of the wife as Christ is the head of the man. "Christ is the head of every man, the head of a woman is her husband, and the Head of Christ is God" (1 Corinthians 11:3). God the Father designed, for our benefit, this order of authority which can be described as "God's umbrella of protection." (See the illustration on the next page.) God's order is as follows:

God the Father

Christ

Man

Woman

Children

Christ, who is God and *equal* with the Father, is subject to the Father. The man is subject to those in authority over him: God, and others such as government officials, police, and employer (though all men are equals). The wife is subject to her husband, though she is his equal. The children are subject to their parents' authority, though they are not inferior beings. God uses this order of authority in the human race to protect and provide us with maximum happiness.

The woman, operating under God's prescribed umbrella of protection for her, assumes her role of supporting and encouraging her husband and caring for her home and children. She also has the freedom to participate in various activities that do not conflict with her role of wife and mother.

The husband's sphere of responsibility under God's umbrella of protection includes his leadership in the home as well as his responsibilities in business and society. Through his position he has the opportunity to develop his masculine God-given strengths and abilities.

As the wife responds to her husband's leadership, she enjoys protection and fulfillment in the position that God designed for her. She does not assume pressures and problems that she is not designed to carry. Through this divine order of authority, God is able to deal directly with both the man and the woman, providing them each with total fulfillment. This fulfillment is denied when the wife leaves her position of responder and gets between her husband and God in a position of leadership.

Your first reaction to God's plan for your husband to rule over you will probably be rebellion. You may have picked up this wrong attitude toward man's authority from your mother. Regardless of the reason for your rebellion, you will not want to pass this sinful attitude on to your children. Confess your rebellion as sin, and trust Jesus Christ to change you. Before I understood that God's plan was for my benefit, I too rebelled against the thought of being totally dependent upon my husband.

When you are having doubts as to how to respond to your husband, remember that the husband-wife relationship is an earthly picture of the relationship between Christ and the Church (believers). Just as the Church is totally dependent on Jesus Christ, so you as a wife are to be totally dependent on your husband. In this atmosphere, you are protected and fulfilled; your husband is inspired to be the man God created him to be; and your children are provided with an ideal atmosphere in which to develop and mature. God's plan is all-inclusive—total provision for everyone. You are totally surrounded by His loving protection, His umbrella (divine order) above and His loving hand underneath. "Though he [the righteous] fall, he shall not be utterly cast down, for the Lord grasps his hand in support and upholds him" (Psalm 37:24).

Roles of the Husband and Wife

Some people think marriage is a 50-50 deal, but it is not. It requires 100% from each partner. Each partner has a role that demands his all. Each role is equal in importance to the other but carries with it different responses and responsibilities. The fact that the roles are different does not mean that one is inferior to the other. Each role is judged in terms of its function and cannot operate efficiently without the other. A husband and wife complement each other in much the same way as a lock and key go together. Either is incomplete without the other.

Our position in God's divine order has nothing to do with our individual worth or importance. Individual worth and *not* respective roles is in view in Galatians 3:28. "There is [now no distinction], neither Jew nor Greek, there is neither slave nor free, there is not male and female; for you are all one in Christ Jesus." A woman tends to differ from a man in her interests, thinking, and abilities, as well as in her body. These distinctions make her the husband's complement, but they do not make her inferior. Neither man nor woman has cause for boasting. Neither needs to fret about having an inferior position.

The roles of the husband and wife could be compared to the offices of president and vice president of an organization. Each party understands, on acceptance of the position, that each office carries with it heavy responsibilities. Since the policies are clearly established, there is never any doubt about who is the president. However, the president's success depends on the vice president's help in carrying out the policies. When new decisions have to be made, the president may consult the vice president for advice, but he assumes responsibility for the final decision.

Once a policy is decided, they work together as a team to carry it out. The president may, if he chooses, delegate some of his authority to the vice president. When the president is gone, he can trust the vice president to carry on as if he himself were there. In this relationship, they share a oneness, good communication, emotional peace, and security, provided the vice president is not struggling to gain control of the organization!

God meant the man's and woman's roles to be different. After all He made them male and female (Genesis 1:27), not unisex. This difference is not only physical but also emotional and temperamental. Masculine traits include the ability to see the overall picture in a situation and to be firm and decisive when solving problems. Womanly traits include the ability to see details of a situation and to contribute valuable insights based on a compassionate, sensitive nature. For instance, as you prepare for a business party, you may be caught up in the details of the party preparation or how to prevent Mrs. X from offending Mrs. Y. Your husband may be thinking in terms of how the party will contribute to his business success for the coming year. By using your respective natural traits, you will be able to work together as a team.

If you do not recognize that God designed you and your husband to complement each other, you may try to force your husband to act and respond to life as you do. Should you succeed, he would have to switch to the feminine role of being the responder, abandoning his masculine responsibilities. If you recognize, however, that by nature your roles are different, you can develop your feminine traits and become a truly feminine woman.

Does My Advice or Opinion Count?

A woman's advice and insights are valuable assets to a man. However, there are some things to consider if your advice is to be effective.

A man will value your advice more highly if he asks for it, which he probably will if you are being a loving, submissive wife. When he asks your opinion, answer him objectively, sticking to the issue and the facts involved. Remember, men tend to use speech to express ideas and communicate factual information, while women have a tendency to use speech to express feelings or vent their emotions. As you give your opinion, try not to express your emotions, but briefly share, on the basis of facts, your thoughts concerning the situation.

Do I have to wait until I am asked to share my opinion? Only if you know your husband does not want unasked-for advice. The judgment, wisdom, and opinion of a loving wife are great assets to a man. To withhold these insights is doing your husband a great injustice. Being submissive does not mean saying nothing; it means putting yourself completely at the disposal of the person who is over you.

Many times a man needs insights or information in order to make a wise decision or to formulate a correct viewpoint. For instance, you are usually more closely involved with your children's activities and friends than your husband is. To aid him in making decisions and establishing policies regarding the children and their activities, you may need to contribute information. Also, you may be able to share insights based on God's Word that will help him avoid or correct a wrong and destructive viewpoint. "The heart of her husband doth safely trust in her [the virtuous woman] . . . She openeth her mouth with wisdom" (Proverbs 31:11, 26, KJV).

The Bible gives an example of a wife who helped her husband correct his point of view. Manoah and his wife had no children. The Angel of the Lord appeared to Mrs. Manoah and told her she would bear a son. This son, Samson, would begin to rescue Israel from the Philistines.

After Manoah's wife told him about the Angel's visit, he prayed that God would send the Angel again to give them more instructions about caring for the child. When the Angel of the Lord did come, Manoah did not recognize Him until He had ascended into heaven. "And Manoah said to his wife, 'We shall surely die, because we have seen God.' But his [sensible] wife said to him, 'If the Lord were pleased to kill us, He would not have received a burnt offering and a cereal offering at our hands, or have shown us all these things, or now have announced such things as these' " (Judges 13:22-23).

A wife can be a great help to her husband by sharing her insights in the proper way. True, she must give him advice in a feminine manner as described in Proverbs 31:26: "She opens her mouth with skillful and godly wisdom, and in her tongue is the law of kindness—giving counsel and instruction."

Ask yourself, "How will my words or actions affect my husband? Will what I say or do in a certain situation jeopardize his position as my leader?" If you consider these questions before you speak or act, you will be more apt to obey the "law of kindness" and will not run the risk of undermining his role as leader.

Never attempt to force your point of view on your husband. Simply say, "I feel this way," or "I believe such and such."

Leave him free to use or not use your advice as he sees best. Your job is to enhance his role as leader, so don't give your advice on a man-to-man basis or with an attitude of authority, superiority, or motherliness. Express your thoughts lovingly, leaving the final decision to your husband, assuring him of your support.

If you feel he is making the wrong decision, you may appeal your case to a higher court (talk to Christ about the situation in prayer and trust Christ for the ultimate outcome). Contributing your advice in this feminine way will relieve you of the burdensome responsibility of the final decision and will give support and encouragement to your husband.

7

Protection for Your Benefit

Under God's umbrella of protection, the husband is God's earthly agent through whom He protects the woman physically, psychologically, and spiritually. His provision is complete.

In what way do you need physical protection? You need protection from laborious tasks as well as from physical attack. Let's face it! It is not likely that you are as strong, muscularly, as a man. "In the same way you married men should live considerately with [your wives], with an intelligent recognition [of the marriage relation], honoring the woman as [physically] the weaker" (1 Peter 3:7). Your husband should protect you from such hard tasks as moving furniture, building fences, repairing automobiles, doing carpentry. Today you also need protection from physical or sexual attack just as your female ancestors did in the wilds of the frontier. When you try to develop the ability to protect yourself, you endanger your femininity.

Sometimes, too, your husband must protect your health by curtailing your many activities. If your husband has complained about your busy schedule, he may be worried about you. He may be expressing his love by saying your health is important to him. Thank him for his concern and let his advice be a reminder that you are doing more than God planned for you to do.

Your husband also protects you physically by providing you with food, clothing, and shelter. This is a sacred obligation given to him by God. "Whoever fails to provide for his own relatives, and especially for those of his immediate family, has disowned the faith and is worse than an unbeliever" (1 Timothy 5:8, wms). This warning was not given to the woman but to the man.

Man's work is a blessing. It provides him with the opportunity to develop his God-given abilities as he faces struggles, burdens, and difficulties for his family. Be careful not to deny your husband the respect, the honor, and the deep satisfaction of fulfilling this role God assigned him: "Make it your ambition and definitely endeavor to live quietly and peacefully, to mind your own affairs, and to work with your hands, as we charged you; so that you may bear yourselves becomingly, be correct and honorable and command the respect of the outside world, being (self-supporting), dependent on nobody and having need of nothing" (1 Thessalonians 4:11-12).

Since God assigned man the responsibility of providing for his family, He rebukes the man who fails to do so, calling him "worse than an unbeliever [who performs his obligation in these matters]" (1 Timothy 5:8).

Even as it is your husband's job to provide the money, so it is your responsibility to support his financial plans. You should willingly make any effort necessary to make the dollar stretch, as described in Proverbs 31:13-14. "She seeks out the wool and flax and works with willing hands to develop it. She is like the merchant ships loaded with foodstuffs, she brings her household's food from a far [country]." You may learn to make the dollars stretch by finding bargains, cooking economical dishes, learning to sew, and by developing many other ideas God will give you.

As you limit your life-style to your husband's salary scale, God will direct your family finances. He will provide for you in a way that will not cause your husband to feel inferior. God may lead a neighbor to give you the very piece of furniture you need or an aunt to mail you the special dress you had prayed for. Too often, by using credit cards, you can limit God and place your family under unnecessary financial strain.

You must be careful never to belittle your husband's producing power. Such comments as *"We* can't afford this," or "I have to skimp and save to make ends meet" will discourage your husband. Try not to comment on the ways in which you have economized in order to help out, even though your economizing pleases you. Your thriftiness is good and will give you a feeling of satisfaction, but telling your husband about it only reminds him that it is necessary because of his limited income. You will help your husband in his role of financial protector by your quiet economy, open support, and gratitude for his provision for you and the family.

Many women have said, "My husband has hinted that I should work outside our home. I am trained in a certain area and we could use the extra money. Should I go to work?" No, it is your husband's job to meet the family's financial obligations. Do not feel guilty for not helping him. As a matter of fact, instead of helping him, you would be damaging his ego.

However, ask yourself why he suggested that you go to work. Is it because you have given him the impression that you are not satisfied with his provision for you? If so, set about to correct the impression you have made. Assure him that you are willing to move to a smaller house or make any other adjustments necessary to ease the financial burden. Any sacrifice on your part will be worth the satisfaction your husband will have, knowing that he can successfully meet his responsibilities.

If he insists that you go to work, take steps to obey him. Meanwhile, pray that God will change his mind or give you an alternate solution. God knows what you and your husband need to mature, so His answer to your prayer will fulfill your current needs.

Of course an emergency may arise. Your husband may become ill or lose his job. You may be forced to look for work to help out financially. The working woman is described in Proverbs 31:24: "She makes fine linen garments and leads others to buy them; she delivers to the merchants girdles [or sashes that free one for service]." Your helping out financially can be done without harm to your husband if you don't give the impression that you are a martyr or a rescuing hero. However, except in emergencies, I do not believe it is God's plan for a wife's work to supplement the family income.

In quite a different set of circumstances, you may find that outside work would be advisable for you. If you have no children, or if they are now grown, a job that does not interfere in any way with your role as a wife may be just the thing for you. Working under these circumstances, or as I do in writing and lecturing, should be an avocation rather than to supplement the family income. Any income from your activity should be incidental, like a bonus.

A good checklist to determine if your activity is within God's plan for you would be:

1. Does your activity conflict or compete with your husband's schedule or your duties as wife or mother?

2. Does your husband feel your activity is more important to you than he is?

3. Does your activity cause you to no longer be financially dependent on your husband?

4. Does your husband still feel the total responsibility of providing for his family?

Threats to you do not stop at the physical level. You also need psychological protection. Your emotions are a wonderful part of your femininity when they express themselves in loving response, appreciation, warmth, or kindness. But when you assume responsibilities that belong to your husband, you often encounter situations that subject you to undue emotional pressure. Your emotional response is then likely to be one of anger, frustration, and hurt. You may mishandle situations because you are so upset, and you may end up behaving like a shrew. This is often the case when you must deal with offensive salesmen, belligerent creditors, irritable neighbors, or even your own inconsiderate teenagers. Your husband is to serve as a protective agent between you and such pressures.

The next time your neighbor complains about your crabgrass getting into his lawn of fescue, simply say, "I'll speak to my husband about it." It's his problem, not yours. Isn't that comforting?

As you fulfill your role, you can even expect your husband to protect you from emotional conflicts with the children. He will demand that they respect you because he is learning to respect and appreciate your real womanhood. You will become like the woman described in Proverbs 31:25: "Strength and dignity are her clothing and her position is strong and secure."

When you do not understand that finances are your husband's responsibility, you may become emotionally upset about how the bills will be paid. However, if there is to be any worry involved, it is your husband's worry, not yours. Men are given the capacity to cope with this pressure. Of course you should be understanding and cooperative.

If you handle the family finances and write the checks, stop and ask yourself, "Why am I doing this?" Your husband has the right to delegate jobs, and it could be that he has requested your help. If he has given you the job of paying the bills, do keep him up to date on the family finances—so he'll know how to plan and spend. But if you are handling the finances in order to control the "purse strings," you are trying to lead. You're usurping your husband's role and will not have God's umbrella of protection.

You are usually least aware of your need for protection in the spiritual realm. Yet this is one of your more vulnerable areas. Being a more emotional creature, you may be deceived into making decisions on the basis of what appeals to you or what appears to be right instead of making decisions based on the principles set forth in God's Word.

Eve's decision to eat the forbidden fruit, for instance, was made on the basis of emotional appeal, and you know the consequences! "It was not Adam who was deceived but [the] woman who was deceived and deluded and fell into transgression" (1 Timothy 2:14). If you do not regulate your life by God's Word, you will be as easily led astray as Eve. "For among them [men who hold a form of godliness but deny its power] are those who worm their way into homes and captivate silly and weak-natured and spiritually dwarfed women, loaded down with [the burden of their] sins, [and easily] swayed and led away by various evil desires and seductive impulses. [These weak women will listen to anybody who will teach them]; they are forever inquiring and getting information, but are never able to arrive at a recognition and knowledge of the Truth" (2 Timothy 3:6-7).

It should be comforting to know that God will, literally, show you His will for your life through your husband. If you have prayed about a certain matter and feel you know God's will concerning it, use God's final check. Ask your husband what you should do. He may say "no" to what you feel God wants you to do, but God can change your husband's mind. The Bible says, "The king's heart is in the hand of the Lord, as the rivers of water; He turneth it whithersoever He will" (Proverbs 21:1, KJV). If God can change a king's mind at will, can't He also cause your husband to go along with the thing that is His plan for you?

You can trust God to lead you and your family spiritually without your defying your husband. When you get out from under God's umbrella of protection and become the spiritual leader in your home at the expense of your husband's headship, everyone suffers. Rebekah, for instance, conspired with her favorite son Jacob to deceive her aged, blind husband Isaac (Genesis 27). Through her deception, Jacob received his twin brother Esau's patriarchal blessing, but much heartache resulted. Esau's murderous hatred banished Jacob from his home for 21 toil-filled years, and Rebekah died without seeing her son again. It seems logical to conclude that her deceit also put a wedge between her and Isaac. God told Rebekah that Jacob would be the master (Genesis 25:23). How unfortunate that she did not trust God to work it out His way.

Your attitude toward your husband reveals your spiritual condition. You are rebellious to Christ's leadership to the same degree that you rebel against your husband's leadership. Sue had trouble accepting this principle until Christ made it very obvious one day. She was working in her flower garden when Bill asked her to empty the garbage can. *Why should I stop what I'm doing to do that?* she thought rebelliously. *I'll do it later, but not now.*

A day or two afterwards, the Holy Spirit prompted Sue to share with her neighbor how she might know Christ personally. Sue's immediate response was, "Lord, I'll do it later, but not now." Yes, her response to Christ was identical to her response to her husband—the one God had put over her.

God planned for your husband to stand between you and the world to protect you from the physical, emotional, and spiritual pressures that are harmful to you. As you allow your husband this privilege, you will begin to experience the pleasure of being a truly feminine woman.

How to Help Your Husband Become the Leader

At first you may say, "Sure, I'm convinced that my husband should be the head of our home, but he simply is not a leader." Remember, God would not command the man to be the leader ("For the husband is the head of the wife as Christ is the Head of the Church," Ephesians 5:23) without giving him the ability. With God's help and yours, your husband can be the leader God meant him to be.

If you have willingly or unwillingly assumed the role of leadership in your home, you can begin to ease out of it by *gradually* transferring to your husband the responsibilities he will most easily accept. When you begin to tell the children, "Go ask Daddy. He is the head of our home," they may be as shocked as their father, but this is a good way to start.

When your display of confidence in his leadership convinces him that his leadership is a permanent arrangement, not a temporary "kick" of yours, he should begin to respond positively. He very likely will enjoy the ego-boosting experience of taking charge and having you and the children follow his advice or decisions. He'll gradually gain confidence in himself and enjoy his new role.

Of course, you may have some reservations about your husband's leadership. "What happens when he makes the wrong decisions?" you may ask. Well, just remember that in trusting your husband, you are actually trusting Jesus Christ. He has promised to direct you through your husband. He can even use your husband's mistakes to teach him—and you—valuable lessons if you will stay under the "umbrella of God's protection." Remember Romans 8:28 says, *"All things* work together for good to them that love God" (KJV).

Suppose your husband has an important business decision to make and asks your advice. You warn against the venture, but he overrules your recommendation and goes ahead. As you predicted, the decision is a mistake. You now have the choice of ruining God's teaching opportunity by saying, "I told you so" or of maintaining a sweet, understanding attitude. If you have the proper attitude in this situation, you both can benefit from his mistake. You may learn, for instance, that you have been putting your trust in money rather than turning to Christ for your security.

As you maintain a sweet attitude and trust God, He will be able to deal with your husband directly and will not have to work against the interference of a nagging wife.

The promise in Romans 8:28 applies to both you and your husband. As you make mistakes (and you will), pray that God will work them out to glorify Him. I keep a button on my dressing table that is a comfort to me. It has these letters on it, "PBPGINFWMY" (Please be patient, God is not finished with me yet). Only God can take our mistakes and turn them into blessings as He makes us like Jesus.

Let go! Relax. You can enjoy the freedom of knowing that, along with the right to make the final decisions, your husband carries the responsibility for the consequences of his decisions. Resist temptations to interfere with his leadership because you feel his decisions or actions are too forceful, harsh, or wrong. Don't argue your point or try to manipulate him. Respond to his leadership in a relaxed manner, and you will find that your husband usually wants to please you.

Each year when they traded in their car, Peggy and Ken debated about whether they would buy the small car Ken wanted or the station wagon Peg wanted. Peggy's persistence usually won. After learning the principle of how to give advice, she simply shared with Ken her desire for a station wagon and left the final decision with him. She was sure he would come home with the small car because, after all, she had not argued or manipulated. Yet she decided to trust God regardless of the outcome, and Ken bought the station wagon.

I don't mean to imply that you will always get your way. Marjorie wanted very much to go to a Sunday School party, but Joe decided they would stay home and watch a football game on TV. Marjorie discovered a greater joy in committing her disappointment to Christ and watching the football game with Joe than she would have if she had gone to the party. Before learning to accept her husband's decisions, Marjorie would have pouted and made the evening miserable for both of them.

You will encourage your husband to take the lead by being a good follower and telling him how much you enjoy his taking charge. As you display trust in his ability, he will be more eager to continue as head of the house. Interestingly, as you follow, your husband will lead; but if you become aggressive, he may regress. You nag, and he will rebel. If you desire to please him, he will want to please you.

Be efficient in fulfilling your responsibilities to your husband, children, and home. Then your roles will be more clearly defined, and your husband will want to apply the same efficiency in his role. One lady commented, "As I have become a better wife, my husband has wanted to be a better husband. He can never be outdone."

Your husband can be head of the house even when he is absent if you faithfully follow his wishes for you and the family. For instance, you may not always agree with him that your teenagers should be home early on weekend nights. Yet you still make sure that they get in at their usual time, even though your husband is away on a business trip. You may tell them, "Dad wants you to be in by 10:30, so be sure to be home by then." Even if your husband is away for an extended time, you and the children can live under his protective leadership. God's provision is marvelous.

Ask God to show you any areas in which you have assumed your husband's role. Then go to him and tell him you have been wrong in assuming the role God has given him. Be specific; name the areas in which you've taken over: disciplining the children, refusing to move when he was offered a promotion, or not following the budget.

Tell him you know that since God gave him this role, God has equipped him to carry it out. Be sure to ask his forgiveness for challenging his abilities by interfering. Ask him to forgive you for your failure. Tell him that you are excited and comforted by the knowledge that God will lead you through him.

8

God's Best for You

Do you want God's best? This is an important question for you to settle. If you receive His best, you will experience *peace* of mind and heart: "Great peace have they who love Your law; nothing shall offend them or make them stumble" (Psalm 119:165). God's *joy,* too, will be yours if you choose His best: "But His joy is in those who reverence Him, those who expect Him to be loving and kind" (Psalm 147:11, LB).

Sarah chose God's best by responding to her husband as her authority. "It was thus that Sarah obeyed Abraham (following his guidance and acknowledging his headship over her by) calling him lord—master, leader, authority" (1 Peter 3:6).

God's best is revealed through His Word: "You are my hiding place and my shield; I hope in Your Word" (Psalm 119:114). As the Word reveals Jesus Christ and His will for you, it will be like a flashlight to illumine the path ahead: "Your Word is a lamp to my feet and a light to my path" (Psalm 119:105).

His Word is permanently established and He will always

honor and fulfill its principles. "Forever, O Lord, Your Word [stands firm as the heavens] is settled in heaven" (Psalm 119:89). "For You have exalted above all else Your name and Your Word, and You have magnified Your Word above all Your name!" (Psalm 138:2) The final authority in your life must be God's Word. His protection of you is based on your doing His will, not your will. "If you want Me to protect you, you must learn to believe what I say" (Isaiah 7:9, LB).

God's Authority for Wives

In His kindness and grace, God makes it clear in His Word that He wants you to obey your husband. "Wives, be subject —be submissive and adapt yourselves—to your own husbands as [a service] to the Lord" (Ephesians 5:22). Many other verses say the same thing. You might like to read them in your Bible: 1 Peter 3:1, 5-6; Genesis 3:16; 1 Corinthians 11:3, 8-9; 1 Timothy 2:11-12; Titus 2:2-4.

The words "be submissive" in Ephesians 5:22 suggest or imply continuous action. Submission is to be a way of life. The wife never stops submitting. Submission is also used in the military sense—a position to which a wife is assigned.

Though God has assigned you that position, you still fulfill it voluntarily. He does not force you to take it any more than he forces you to receive His Son as your Saviour. The phrase "as unto the Lord" keeps this act of submission from being slavery and makes it a voluntary act of love. You willingly submit to your husband because you love the Lord and want to obey and please Him, not because you fear Him.

When you willingly, lovingly submit to your husband, your spirit of gentleness and love inspires your husband to treat you gently and to cherish and protect you.

Notice, however, that none of the verses listed say, "Be submissive if your husband is right, if he is a Christian, or if you can understand the outcome." No, God applies no such exceptions to your obedience to your husband.

Have you ever heard of a woman having a problem agreeing with the commandment, "You shall not steal"? (See Exodus 20:15.) Perhaps some do, but I myself have never heard one say, "It is all right to steal *if* you are hungry, *if* no one sees you, or *if* you strongly desire an object." God undoubtedly did not intend for us to steal. We accept this because He has made it clear. Yet, frequently women who would never consider stealing reject God's commandment to submit to their husbands. If you are such a woman and are unwilling to give God your total obedience, do not allow the Lord to be discredited by the blunders your disobedience produces. Admit you are living according to your plan, not His.

Most women I talk with do want to be God's women and be in His will. However, you can be in the center of His will only if you obey the one God has put in authority over you—your husband. You display your obedience to God through being subject to your husband. To refuse to recognize your husband's authority makes your life incomplete and unsatisfying—a direct result of breaking God's commandment relating to this issue. Remember, you do not degrade yourself or place yourself in an inferior position when you recognize and respect his authority. Instead, you gain dignity, fulfillment, femininity, and freedom to be the woman God wants you to be. God's plan is designed for your benefit.

Does complete obedience to Jesus Christ through your husband frighten you? "The Lord is fair in everything He does, and full of kindness" (Psalm 145:17, LB). Jesus Christ's love for you is so great and complete, it is hard to understand. "But God shows and clearly proves His [own] love for us by the fact that while we were still sinners, Christ, the Messiah, the Anointed One, died for us" (Romans 5:8). After dying for you, Jesus would not play a dirty trick by putting you in a position to make you miserable.

Do not put His love on the level of or below man's love (which you do when you feel that He would repay obedience with punishment). "Or what man is there of you, if his son asks him for a loaf of bread, will hand him a stone? Or if he asks for a fish, will hand him a serpent? If you then, evil as you are, know how to give good and advantageous gifts to your children, how much more will your Father who is in heaven [perfect as He is] give good and advantageous things to those who keep on asking Him!" (Matthew 7:9-11)

Suppose, to use a common illustration, that when I return home after a trip, my sons greet me with these words, "Mother, we've missed you and have decided that we'll do anything you want us to do, starting now."

Would I respond with, "Oh, good. I'm going to make your life miserable. You'll have brussels sprouts three times a day, and you'll never get to do anything you like to again. You'll be sorry you made such a commitment to me."

Of course I wouldn't say that. Once I finished hugging my sons, I'd probably go out and buy them the things they'd wanted. If we, in our incomplete human love, respond this way, surely we should not expect less from God. His love is perfect. He reaches out, wanting to minister to us in our deepest needs. If we can trust each other, surely we can trust the God of love and salvation. "We need have no fear of Someone who loves us perfectly; His perfect love for us eliminates all dread of what He might do to us. If we are afraid, it is for fear of what He might do to us, and shows that we are not fully convinced that He really loves us. So you see, our love for Him comes as a result of His loving us first" (1 John 4:18-19, LB).

It should comfort you to know that God's will for you is obedience to your husband.

The Wife's Protection
Since God states in Ephesians 5:24 (NASB) that "as the

Church is subject to Christ, so also the wives ought to be to their husbands in everything," do not think you are an exception. You may immediately say, "You don't know my husband! He's unsaved. He's unreasonable. That may work for some husbands and wives but not for us."

God deals with this specific problem in Scripture: "In the same way, you wives, be submissive to your own husbands so that even if any of them are disobedient to the Word they may be won without a word by the behavior of their wives, as they observe your chaste and respectful behavior" (1 Peter 3:1-2, NASB). Obviously, the Lord is talking here to the woman whose husband is unsaved.

Your submission to your husband is part of God's plan for order in our world (see 1 Peter 2:13-18). The words "in the same way" in 1 Peter 3:1 refer back to verses 13-14 and 18 in the previous chapter. "Submit yourselves for the Lord's sake to every human institution: whether to a king as the one in authority; or to governors, as sent by Him" (vv. 13-14), and "Servants, be submissive to your masters with all respect, not only to those who are good and gentle, but also to those who are unreasonable" (v. 18).

God is saying that His plan for you is submission to the one in authority over you—daily joyful submission to your husband even as you would submit to governments or a master. So if you allow the Lord to cleanse you, fill you, and control you, and if you take a position of wholehearted submission to your husband because God has said you should, you can depend on God to fulfill His Word in caring for you and helping you carry out His command.

Remember 1 Corinthians 10:13? "You haven't been tempted more than you could expect. And you can trust God; He will not let you be tested more than you can stand. But when you are tested, He will also make a way out so that you can bear it" (BECK). Now you don't know *how* God will fulfill His Word. You simply trust that He *will*. If your husband has asked you to do something unreasonable, God may change your husband's mind. As we noted earlier, "The king's heart [and your husband's!] is in the hand of the Lord, as the rivers of water, He turneth it whithersoever He will" (Proverbs 21: 1, KJV).

Perhaps examples from life will help you understand God's gracious way of working things out for you when you obey Him and honor your husband.

Barbara had become a Christian, but her husband, Don, had not. She began to attend church faithfully and even took the children. Don seemed bewildered at first by her new faith and her interest in church. Then he became jealous and hurt because she was spending her Sundays away from him. He did not feel as if he was number one in her life anymore.

Some weeks had gone by when Barbara heard these principles of the wife's submission to her husband whether he was a Christian or not. She wanted to please the Lord, so she decided to concentrate on honoring her husband. Easter Sunday morning came, and she and the children were all ready to go to church when Don woke up.

Right away, Barbara sensed that Don was unhappy. "Honey, would you like me to stay home with you today?" she asked. "You know I want you to be happy. If you'd prefer to have me and the children home with you, we'll stay here." He didn't answer, but she could tell that he wanted her to stay home.

She and the children changed into more casual clothes, and she planned some relaxed games for the children. As the morning progressed, her husband's mood got better and better. Later in the day, Don called the children to him. He picked up the Bible and said, "Children, I want us to read some of the Bible together." He read from Proverbs and talked to them about what God said.

Naturally, Barbara's heart was warmed. She had given her husband his rightful place, and he was no longer jealous of her relationship with the church and Jesus Christ. Here he was taking the spiritual leadership, and he wasn't a Christian! Actually, the day ended up being far better than an Easter service because the family was united in reading and discussing God's Word together. Now, a year later, Don is a Christian too. True, there were times when Barbara had to stay home from church simply to give her husband his place in her life. But he might not have received Christ if she had not considered him.

Allison had an experience much like Barbara's. Only Allison had been raised to believe that churchgoing was the absolute right thing. When the church doors were open, you went. She was quite self-righteous about attending. But Allison had married a man who did not love Christ and did not care to attend church.

Allison's Sunday School teacher began to teach these biblical principles about the wife's role of submission. One Sunday she got Allison aside and told her, "Your husband simply doesn't understand what's going on in your life. He's jealous. He cannot understand spiritual truths, and if he wants you to stay home with him, then you should, until he is assured of his rightful place in your heart."

Allison was shocked. She had never heard anything like that before. But when she saw that the principles of submission came right from God's Word, she agreed to try them.

The next Sunday, Allison got herself and the children ready for church as usual. Her husband Andy, a traveling salesman, was sleeping late. He awoke, and seeing her getting ready for church, began to rave and curse and tell her he didn't see any difference in church people's lives or any good reason for her attending. Allison very quietly changed into a casual dress.

"What are you doing?" Andy asked in amazement.

"Well, it's obvious you don't want me to go to church," she said. "And I do love you. And I want you to be happy. After all, I haven't spent much time with you since you've been going out of town. So it would be the right thing for me to stay home with you. I'd like to hear what you've been doing this week, anyway."

Andy got out of bed and put his arms around her with tears in his eyes.

Allison said that for the first time that morning she saw something in him she had never seen before—just because she put herself in the position God intended. God was able to bring out qualities in Andy she didn't even know existed. They had a happy day together.

As the weeks went by, Andy began attending church with her and the children. The last I heard, he still hadn't received Christ as Saviour, but he was still attending church with his family and encouraging them to do so—all because Allison's relationship with Christ and her church were no longer a threat to him.

Men don't really want to be brutal or tyrannical. They act that way because they feel insecure in their relationships with their wives and are fighting desperately to gain the position God meant them to have. Once a man sees he doesn't have to fight for his wife's love, that he has her obedience, and her full attention, he in turn will allow her to have her own activities and interests—so long as she doesn't take advantage.

Now, as I said before, you don't know how God is going to work in your particular situation. Perhaps your husband won't change in the way Don and Andy did.

Laura's Jake gave her a bad time when she told him she was going to obey him and put him first in a way she hadn't before. He was not a Christian and decided to test her.

"OK, Laura, let's go to the Royal Three tonight." (It was a nightclub that featured lewd entertainment.)

Laura was shaken but didn't show Jake how she felt. "I said I'd do what you want me to, so I will," she told him.

He couldn't believe her and kept saying, "Well, what will you do when such and such happens?"

"I'll do what you say," she told him and proceeded to get ready. They were all dressed and ready to leave when he suddenly got a blinding headache. "Honey, I can't go," he told her. And they didn't. God had intervened.

Marilyn's husband also asked her to go to a nightclub with him and she went. However, she graciously refrained from taking part in some of the activities in such a way that she did not make her husband feel uncomfortable. Another woman, also sitting by and watching, noticed that Marilyn wasn't taking part and came over to talk to her. Marilyn explained that she was refraining from the activities because of her faith in Jesus Christ. So Marilyn was able to glorify her Saviour even at a nightclub.

Sally's problem wasn't so overwhelming. The family was visiting her mother one day. Her mother had some nice rich dirt and offered Sally some for her plants at home. Sally got a big bucket and filled it full. But as she started to put it in the car, her husband George, said, "You're not going to take that home in our clean car!"

"Why, George, I can put paper on the floor and hold the bucket so it won't spill," Sally answered.

"No, I don't want a dirty pail in the car," he told her. And that was that. Sally didn't argue because she knew these principles of submitting to her husband. She figured she'd come back later in the truck and get the dirt, and just forgot about the incident. But as they were getting ready to leave, her husband surprised her. "Oh, go ahead and get the bucket of dirt," he said. "If you hold it like you promised, it should be OK."

This little incident made Sally think back to other times in their relationship. She realized that George felt at times as if he were no longer the head of the house. She could see that when he felt sure of himself and not threatened, he was as sweet as pie.

So many marriage problems result from a misunderstanding of the husband-wife relationship or from the wife's deliberate refusal to submit to her husband. It is significant that six verses in 1 Peter 3:1-7 speak to the wife about her role and only one verse instructs the husband. The woman's role is crucial, strategic, and it is a hard role to fill. God takes extra time, giving instructions to the woman on how she is to fulfill that role so she won't go to an extreme and become a slave but will still retain her individuality and her husband's love.

Basically, the woman's protection is God's Word. God has outlined in His Word the fact that he wants her to obey her husband without exception. If she does, she can depend on God to keep His Word and to deal with her husband in whatever way He sees necessary to enable the woman to do what He wants her to do.

The Wife's Responsibility

Your attitude toward God and your husband is the key to your success with God and man. If you do not want to submit to your husband, confess this to the Lord. Trust Him to control your life and change your desires. You will be thrilled to see God's Word become a living reality in your mind.

God holds you responsible for your attitude and motives. You must be transparent before Him. He cannot be fooled. "For the Lord sees not as man sees; for man looks on the outward appearance, but the Lord looks on the heart" (1 Samuel 16:7). Do not attempt to rationalize or justify your actions. "We can justify our every deed, but God looks at our motives" (Proverbs 21:2, LB). It is relaxing and comforting to be open and honest before God. He loves you!

You cannot play games with your husband either. He can

sense if you obey willingly or grudgingly. Do not be like the little boy whose daddy told him to sit down in the seat while riding in the car. The little boy refused. Finally, the father threatened to stop the car and spank him if he would not obey. The boy sat down but mumbled under his breath, "I'll sit down, but I'm still standing up on the inside." You cannot afford to "stand up on the inside." Such rebellion will destroy your joy and your husband's.

Remember, your husband's unreasonable demands or actions, whether he is saved or not, can be stimulated or minimized by your attitude. That is why it is so important for you to voluntarily obey him with pure motives. (Of course, the prerequisite to a right relationship with your husband is a right relationship with God, free from unconfessed sin.)

God's Word reminds us that husbands may be won to the Lord "when they observe the pure and modest way in which you conduct yourselves, together with your reverence [for your husband. That is, you are to feel for him all that reverence includes]—to respect, defer to, revere him; [revere means] to honor, esteem (appreciate, prize), and [in the human sense] adore him; [and adore means] to admire, praise, be devoted to, deeply love and enjoy [your husband]" (1 Peter 3:2).

In other words, your husband will see that you don't fall apart over the things that used to upset you. He observes that when he stays out all night and gives you no reason, you don't go into a tailspin or tantrum or nag him for days. You give him his freedom and accept him the way he is. He sees that you do not give "way to hysterical fears" (1 Peter 3:6), and you have more patience with the children. You're more thoughtful. You're considerate of him; you listen to him; you think about him; you respect him. You reverence him, adore him, admire him, praise him, and enjoy his company.

When your husband sees and lives with this kind of woman, he cannot help but be influenced! He cannot help but be softened and stimulated to be the man that God meant him to be. So it is your responsibility as a wife to fulfill the role God designed for you, keeping your relationship with your husband right and leaving everything else to God. Trust God to deal with your husband and work out difficulties in the way He sees best. God longs for you to trust Him.

What About My Reputation?

The wise woman will fix her mind on obeying God as we have discussed. Her first consideration is to build a successful marriage, not to look around and see what others think about what she's doing or to regulate her life to please others. In other words, if in obeying your husband and putting him first, you must attend a nightclub with him, do not worry about what others will say. Nor should you worry if you can't be in church every Sunday as you would like to be. In other words, do not be concerned about gossips or listen to well-meaning advice, even when it comes from Christian friends.

Some Christians will be very upset if you do not attend church faithfully. They will quote Hebrews 10:25 to you, where it says you should not neglect assembling together for worship. If they are critical, simply tell them you are only refraining for a time so you can later return to church with your husband's blessing, and, hopefully, with him.

Of course, you should study your Bible faithfully, so God can speak to you and guide you when you cannot get to church. You might even ask a friend to tape the Sunday services so you can enjoy them during the week. You may also attend a daytime women's Bible study or find other opportunities to assemble for Christian fellowship. Thus you will not be breaking God's command in Hebrews by submitting to your husband, so don't let anyone tell you that you are.

Your responsibility is to do the will of God, not to seek approval from others. Jesus Christ said, "I can of Mine own self do nothing: as I hear, I judge: and My judgment is just; because I seek not Mine own will, but the will of the Father which hath sent Me" (John 5:30, KJV). If Jesus could say that He had come to do God's will, not His own, certainly you should put God's will first in your life, too.

Jesus' reputation was not very good in some religious circles. Some religious people accused Him of being a drunk (see Luke 7:34, NASB). Others said, "What kind of Man is this that keeps company with tax collectors, prostitutes, and sinners?" (See Matt. 11:19.) Jesus "made Himself of no reputation, and took upon Him the form of a servant, and was made in the likeness of men" (Philippians 2:7, KJV).

Mary, the mother of Jesus, had a bad reputation among those who did not believe in the virgin birth. It has been said that one of the reasons Joseph took Mary with him to Bethlehem the year of Jesus' birth was to protect Mary from gossip at home. Even today some call Jesus the illegitimate son of Mary.

We belong to Jesus Christ. We can trust Him to care for us—His property. "He restoreth my soul; He leadeth me in the paths of righteousness for *His name's sake*" (Psalm 23:3, KJV). It is His reputation that is at stake when you obey Him and your husband, not yours.

Shadows in the Dark

Many questions and fears are the product of your imagination and worries. Do not become upset about someone else's situation or some unknown possibility. Jesus promises to be sufficient for all those who trust in Him for their *present* problems. "God is faithful—reliable, trustworthy, and [therefore] ever true to His promise, and He can be depended on; by Him you were called into companionship and participation with His Son, Jesus Christ our Lord" (1 Corinthians 1:9). Worry about "what ifs" is a sin. "Casting the whole of your care—all your anxieties, all your worries, all your concerns, once and for all —on Him; for He cares for you affectionately, and cares about you watchfully" (1 Peter 5:7). Let the light of Jesus Christ dissolve all your fears or "shadows in the dark"!

Guidelines in Accomplishing God's Will

Your role of submission to your husband will become an exciting adventure when you realize that one of the reasons for this role is to develop a mature attitude in you. God's desire for His children is that they become like Jesus Christ. "For from the very beginning God decided that those who came to Him—and all along He knew who would—should become like His Son, so that His Son would be the First, with many brothers" (Romans 8:29, LB). God wants to use any situation in which you find yourself to make you like Jesus.

Is there any area in which you are having problems with your husband? Has it occurred to you that those problems may be the result of some immaturity in you? Every person has a strong will (OSN). When the OSN is in control of your life, your marriage will be unhappy. God may use either a forceful husband or a husband who withdraws, leaving you with his responsibilities, to break your will.

"Even so consider yourselves also dead to sin and your relation to it broken" (Romans 6:11). When we exchange our desires for Christ's, the initial pain of dying to self is a healing pain which is followed by peace and fulfillment. When we are unwilling to exchange our desires for Christ's, we experience a kind of pain which produces heartaches.

Jesus Christ never promised a problem-free life. "The good man does not escape all troubles—he has them too. But the Lord helps him in each and every one" (Psalm 34:19, LB). These problems are for our benefit. "The punishment You gave me was the best thing that could have happened to me, for it taught me to pay attention to Your laws. They are more valuable to me than millions in silver and gold! Your faithfulness extends to every generation, like the earth You created; it endures by Your decree, for everything serves Your plans" (Psalm 119:71-72, 90-91, LB).

Another guideline to consider is your husband's position. He is a tool in the Father's hand. You are to honor and respect his position, not necessarily his personality. Your husband may not understand you and may have personality deficiencies that bother you, but God promises that He is able to work through these deficiencies if your attitude pleases Him. "When a man's ways please the Lord, He makes even his enemies to be at peace with him" (Proverbs 16:7). If God can enable you to live with an enemy peacefully, He certainly can help you live at peace with an ornery husband.

When a problem comes up, ask yourself, "What is God saying to me through this situation?" We miss many valuable lessons by not responding in this way to difficulties.

Jesus Christ had to take me through a particular lesson many times before I saw what He wanted to teach me. DeWitt had often expressed his disapproval of my talking on the phone frequently while he was home. I thought he was being unfair. Finally, the Lord got through to me and showed me that my behavior expressed more concern for the feelings of others than for my husband. Realizing what my actions implied, I saw how wrong I was. My stubbornness in not seeing earlier what God wanted to teach me, had caused much unnecessary friction. God sees weak areas in our lives—areas we are often unaware of—and wants to help us. The psalmist said, "For all my ways are (fully known) before You" (Psalm 119:168).

Something else that will help you submit to your husband is to find out what his real motive is. This will help you be a helpmate to him. For instance, why doesn't he want you to buy the dress you are so crazy about? Does he want to hurt you or is he considering the family budget?

Some men are addicted to such things as drugs, alcohol, or gambling. The urge to gamble, the need for a fix, or drunkenness may make him unreasonable. Should you obey him under such circumstances?

If your husband drinks or has some other habit that affects his reason, find out what his basic goals are or his wishes in specific instances and obey these, not his unreasonable demands when drunk or obsessed. You are not disobeying him in this instance but are carrying out instructions he has given you when thinking clearly.

Bill was a gambler and seemed to have no control over his desire to gamble. At times he would win tremendous sums of money, but other times, he lost everything he had. Finally, he realized that his gambling could hurt his wife and children and himself. One day, right after winning a large sum of money, he went to his lawyer and had him put the winnings in savings. "I want you to draw up some kind of contract that says I can never touch this money. It's for my children's future and any immediate needs my wife might have," he told the lawyer. "If I come to you on my knees, begging you to break the contract and get the money, don't listen to me."

Later he did go to his wife and beg her to get some of the money out of savings, but she refused, knowing that in his "right frame of mind" he did not want her to touch that money except in real need.

God the Holy Spirit will enable you to be creative in responding to situations. You'll be surprised at the alternatives He will give you in following your husband's directions while maintaining personal convictions.

Coming home tired from work, your husband may say, "Tell anyone who calls that I'm not home."

What is his motive for asking you to say this? Obviously, he does not want to be disturbed; it isn't that he means to

Wed 8:45   chpt 5 and 6
            Nov 3rd   No meeting
    Homework : Bring notebook

- Try to encourage
  Ask god to
- Give his enthusiasm to me in
  my marriage

Ephesians 3:20   Cherrlyn Ferro
Romans 8:28   2748 Bellagh Av
Proverbs 14:1   Bellmore, NY 11710
                    (516) 785-4137

Read Genesis 16
              21:1-21
    Think about ways Sarah
took leadership

    Prayer request

- Maria's friend Andrea has
  breast cancer.
- Nicole's sister
  Tabatha pregnant with cervical
  cancer.
- Diane's friend Pat & her marriage

Suanne's sister contemplating Divorce

9/28

Qualities I wish we/I changed in me.
   1 - over emotional/less emotional
   2. - more enthusiastic
   3. more creative
   4.

How can God use these for
his benefit.

Teach me to lean on others and
God. Find strength in God.

1. NO
2. Yes
3. NO
4. Yes
5. Yes
6. NO
7. NO
8. Yes
9. Yes
10. Yes
11. Yes

force you to lie. Therefore, you can tell him that you'll be glad to handle the calls so that he won't be disturbed. You can respond to those who call with, "May I have your name and number? My husband will call when it's convenient."

Choose your wording carefully when responding creatively to your husband's requests. Your response must not project any disapproval of him or make him feel guilty. Obedience to God's Word will help develop your common sense and good judgment. "Now teach me good judgment as well as knowledge. For Your laws are my guide" (Psalm 119:66, LB).

When your husband has made a wrong decision, remember that God is bigger than he or your circumstances, so give God time to change your husband's mind. Remember, "Just as water is turned into irrigation ditches, so the Lord directs the king's thoughts. He turns them wherever He wants to" (Proverbs 21:1, LB). "He changes the times and the seasons, He removes kings and sets up kings, He gives wisdom to the wise and knowledge to those who have understanding!" (Daniel 2:21)

Do not be surprised at what God may use to change your husband's mind! After DeWitt decided to purchase a motorcycle, several months elapsed before God changed his mind about it. God used this period of time to teach me about His faithfulness. Without too much difficulty, I had been able to trust Christ for DeWitt's buying and riding a motorcycle himself, but when he talked of buying a minibike for the boys, I felt he was going too far!

I exercised my privilege of sharing my feelings about the many dangers of cycling. He seemed to agree, and I thought the matter was settled. Later, however, he exercised his right to overrule my decision and bought the boys a minibike. I knew my part was to accept his decision and trust God for the results. I placed the boys' safety in God's hands and, by faith, entered into their joy.

Weeks later, DeWitt had a freak accident as he rode into our driveway one evening. He hurt his knee just enough to convince him of the dangers of cycling. It was his decision to sell the motorcycle three days later. It was also his decision not to repair an unexpected hole that appeared soon afterward in the minibike motor. When God changes one's mind, He does it completely.

Expect pressure while God is working to change your husband's mind. Your husband may give you a bad time just to see if you really intend to support a decision of his that you disagree with. Trust Christ's sufficiency through such pressures. "Bless the Lord who is my immovable rock. He gives me strength and skill in battle. He is always kind and loving to me; He is my fortress, my tower of strength and safety, my deliverer. He stands before me as a shield. He subdues my people under me" (Psalm 144:1-2, LB). God will use these very pressures to develop strong character in you. "We can rejoice, too, when we run into problems and trials for we know that they are good for us—they help us learn to be patient. And patience develops strength of character in us and helps us trust God more each time we use it until finally our hope and faith are strong and steady" (Romans 5:3-4, LB).

Each member of your family can develop strong character through problems and trials just as you do. Many times you do more harm than good by overly protecting your loved ones. They can learn valuable lessons through mistakes, suffering or trouble that they cannot learn any other way. Don't rob them of such opportunities.

When you "delight yourself also in the Lord . . . He will give you the desires and sacred petitions of your heart. Commit your way to the Lord—roll and repose [each care of] your road on Him; trust (lean on, rely on, and be confident) also in Him, and He will bring it to pass" (Psalm 37:4-5). The key is to delight yourself in the *Lord,* not in *your* desires. We must operate according to God's plan and timetable, not ours.

Be prepared! God may change your desires. Recently we bought new bedroom furniture. I wanted a nightstand, too, but DeWitt said we did not need one. My immediate response was one of rebellion. Then I committed my desire to the Lord. When I did, God changed my desire to correspond with De-Witt's. One cannot lose in God's plan.

As you apply these insights and are totally obedient to your husband "as unto the Lord," you can share David's response to the Lord. "How great He is! His power is absolute! His understanding is unlimited" (Psalm 147:5, LB).

Summary of Submission

God wants to use authority to expose our hearts so that we can make progress on the road to maturity. Our response to authority can be a vertical test to see if we want to hear from God, are willing to lay down our way for His way, and are willing to let Him surprise us with His protection and blessings.

Watchman Nee in his book, *Spiritual Authority,* does a thorough treatment on this subject for further study. He makes a statement with which I agree and feel sums up this issue: SUBMISSION IS ABSOLUTE—OBEDIENCE IS RELATIVE. A scriptural incident that illustrates this point is in Daniel 3. Shadrach, Meshach, and Abednego were submissive as expressed in their hearts, words, and actions to the king who made an ungodly request. They submitted to authority even to being thrown into the fiery furnace yet they did not obey the king's ungodly request. Submission is an attitude. Submission is having our hearts and motives pure, yielded, surrendered, abandoned to our God. When these three Hebrew men manifested a submissive spirit, their Lord met them in a special way. See Daniel 3:25.

9

Fadeless Beauty

Most women would give anything to have a beauty that grows instead of fading as they mature. Yet that kind of beauty is the inheritance of every woman who belongs to Christ. God describes this beauty in 1 Peter 3:4: "But let it be the inward adorning and beauty of the hidden person of the heart, with the incorruptible and unfading charm of a gentle and peaceful spirit, which (is not anxious or wrought up, but) is very precious in the sight of God." Incorruptible or fadeless beauty begins on the inside, and its radiance actually transforms your outward appearance.

You can get hung up on unchangeable features you consider ugly, such as a large nose or ears, a long face, or extreme height. When tempted to worry over such characteristics, remember that you had them when your husband chose you. Those features are unimportant to him because they are part of the whole you he loves. Thank God for them, knowing that they have a purpose in God's plan for your life. As you trust Him, he will use those very features to your benefit.

The sparkle in your eyes, a warm smile, a radiant, fresh,

feminine manner, and a gentle, peaceful spirit mean more to your man than your external features. Fadeless beauty is what a mature man looks for in a wife. Men do have different tastes, of course. One may choose a quiet, shy woman, another a dashing, outgoing woman, and still another the dramatic or glamorous type. But the basic characteristics of beauty are the same. Fadeless beauty satisfies the woman who possesses it as well as those around her.

Your inner beauty will be evident only when you realize that you are worthwhile and valuable. You are not "second-rate." You are royalty—a daughter of the King! "You were freed from the worthless life you inherited from your fathers not by a payment of silver or gold which perish, but by the precious blood of Christ, the Lamb without a fault or a spot" (1 Peter 1:18-19, BECK). Being aware of your true value because of what Christ has done for you, will enable you to gain self-respect and self-esteem. Those around you will, in turn, have the same respect for you.

The source of your incorruptible beauty is the spiritual condition of your heart: "For as he thinks in his heart, so is he" (Proverbs 23:7). A gentle nature and peaceful outlook will be mirrored in your eyes and registered on your features just as if your face were a sensitive cardiograph. Lovely attitudes dominating your heart will show up as pleasant expressions on your face. Sparkling eyes, a warm smile, and relaxed facial muscles are symptoms of a good "heart" condition. In contrast, dull eyes, harsh lines of the lips, and a scowl are symptoms of a bad "heart" condition. And the condition of the heart can be altered by only One—Jesus Christ, the Master Physician.

You were meant to be beautiful! Your Heavenly Father wants you, as a daughter of the King, to be especially appealing. As the psalmist says: "So will the King desire your beauty for He is your Lord; be submissive, and reverence and honor

Him. The King's daughter in the inner part of the palace is all glorious!" (Psalm 45:11, 13)

God's Beauty Salon

Your beauty will develop as you maintain a daily appointment with God in His "beauty salon." His beauty treatment is available without cost to all who want fadeless beauty and come to Him for treatment. Treatment involves regular Bible study, obedience to the principles He reveals through study, and talking with Him in prayer.

As God begins your treatment, realize that your natural thoughts and ways of doing things are opposed to His thoughts and ways. Your thoughts are influenced by the world system and your OSN which is opposed to God. "For My thoughts are not your thoughts, neither are your ways My ways, saith the Lord. For as the heavens are higher than the earth, so are My ways higher than your ways, and My thoughts than your thoughts" (Isaiah 55:8-9, KJV).

God works to develop your beauty as you surrender to Him much as you would surrender to the hands of a local beauty operator. "Let the beauty and delightfulness and favor of the Lord our God be upon us" (Psalm 90:17). His beauty treatment involves sitting under His beauty lamp and letting it clear up the defects in your life—transforming the darkness in your soul to the light of beauty.

In Ephesians 4:17-18 (KJV), our natural, sinful state is called darkness: "Walk not as other Gentiles walk, in the vanity of their mind, having the understanding darkened, being alienated from the life of God through the ignorance that is in them." The only solution to this darkness (wrong thoughts, attitudes, and actions) is the transforming light of Jesus Christ which produces true beauty. Jesus said, "I am the Light of the world. He who follows Me will not be walking in the dark, but will have the Light which is Life" (John 8:12).

You may think, "Jesus Christ is no longer present on earth in bodily form to be my light." You are right. He is now "seated at the right hand of the throne of God" (Hebrews 12:2). Yet though Jesus Christ is presently at the right hand of the Father, He has left total provision for you through His Word. He is the Living Word: "In the beginning [before all time] was the Word [Christ], and the Word was with God, and the Word was God Himself" (John 1:1).

Christ has left the Word, His thoughts in writing, to give us direction and to show us His will. He, the Living Word, will make His written Word alive to us so that we will know how to apply it to our individual situation. His Word is a personal letter to us. He promises, "We have the mind of Christ, the Messiah, and do hold the thoughts (feelings and purposes) of His heart" (1 Corinthians 2:16). As we look to Jesus, He will give us wisdom and relation to know Him better. See Ephesians 1:17.

His Word (wisdom) as described in Proverbs 4:9 "shall give to your head a wreath of gracefulness; a crown of beauty and glory." As you read it, you must decide whether or not you will believe it. If your response is positive, God the Holy Spirit, who lives in believers, will use this knowledge to illuminate your soul or inner self. The light of God's Word will chase away the gloom of sin, cleansing you and making you like Jesus Christ. "You are cleansed and pruned already, because of the Word which I have given you—the teachings I have discussed with you" (John 15:3).

If you say no to God's Word, the principle may remain in your mind as intellectual knowledge, but it will not transform you. But if you allow Christ's mind to be formed in your own, and you operate on the basis of God's principles, you will experience stability, inner peace, fulfillment, and beauty. Furthermore, Christ said, "If you live in Me—abide vitally united to Me—and My words remain in you and continue to live in your hearts, ask whatever you will and it shall be done for you" (John 15:7).

You can know whether you are saying yes or no to God's Word by your application or lack of application of God's Word to your daily situations. For instance, God says in 1 Peter 5:7 that you are not to worry but are to let Him take care of your problems. If you refuse to give Him your problems, saying, "Anyone would be upset in my situation," or "It's my nature to worry," you are living according to man's principles for life, not God's (see accompanying diagram on the next page).

God's Word can keep you panic proof as you realize that He has provided for every circumstance in your life. "He knows about everyone, everywhere. Everything about us is bare and wide open to the all-seeing eyes of our living God; nothing can be hidden from Him to whom we must explain all that we have done" (Hebrews 4:13, LB).

He not only knows all things but has already provided victory for you over every situation you will ever face (1 Corinthians 10:13; 15:57). And His light is sufficient for all of life's paths: "Thy Word is a lamp unto my feet and a light unto my path" (Psalm 119:105, KJV).

God's Word is also like a mirror, in that it reveals the defects in your beauty (James 1:23-26). Those defects or sins grieve the Holy Spirit (Ephesians 4:30) and dim your transforming light of beauty. Confession (see 1 John 1:9) returns the Holy Spirit to full control so that the light (Word) can shine into all areas of your life and transform you into the image of Jesus Christ. "I beseech you therefore, brethren, by the mercies of God, that ye present your bodies a living sacrifice, holy, acceptable unto God, which is your reasonable service. And be not conformed to this world; but be ye transformed by the renewing of your mind, that ye may prove what is that good, . . . and perfect will of God" (Romans 12:1-2, KJV).

ROMANS 12: 1-2

or

Are you being
Transformed
into
JESUS CHRIST'S
IMAGE?

SOUL

HUMAN SPIRIT
(Made alive Godward
at salvation)

Conformed
to
WORLD?

Trying to
influence
you

(DIVINE
VIEWPOINT)
BIBLE
"LIGHT"

MIND-THOUGHTS
WILL-DECISIONS
EMOTIONS-FEELINGS

(HUMAN
VIEWPOINT)
WORLD
Satan in
charge
Eph. 2:2

DIVINE VIEWPOINT: Living according to God's principles
(as taught in the Bible)

HUMAN VIEWPOINT: Living according to man's principles (as taught
in mass media and by other individuals)
= Storage area for principles by which we live

Prayer is also an important part of God's beauty treatment.
Jesus said, "If ye abide in Me, and My words abide in you, ye
shall ask what ye will, and it shall be done unto you" (John
15:7, KJV). He also said, "Hitherto have ye asked nothing in
My name; ask, and ye shall receive, that your joy may be full"
(John 16:24, KJV).

As you share your praise, your requests, and your needs with God in prayer in Jesus' name, God promises to hear and answer and fill you with joy. And joy can transform the plainest face into a radiant one.

True, some conditions must be met if prayer is to be answered. If you harbor unconfessed sin, God will not hear you (see Psalm 66:18) and your joy will disappear. But you can pray with King David, "Create in me a clean heart, O God, and renew a right spirit within me. Restore unto me the joy of Thy salvation, and uphold me with Thy free spirit" (Psalm 51:10, 12, KJV). If you refuse to hear God's Word, your prayers will not be acceptable to God. "He who turns away his ear from listening to the law, even his prayer is an abomination" (Proverbs 28:9, NASB).

God also says, "Pray without ceasing" (1 Thessalonians 5:17, KJV). Pray about everything (see Philippians 4:6-7), and you will know His peace—another wonderful beauty aid.

Certainly if you spend time in God's beauty salon, reading His Word and letting it do its work in your life, and if you take time to pray, God's radiance will shine in your face and personality. There is no beauty like that.

Deadly Traps that Mar Beauty

The beauty that God is creating in you and revealing through you, can be marred when anger, fear, or depression control your life. Carnal emotions cannot control you without damaging your beauty and your physical and spiritual health. Medical doctors have estimated that these emotions produce 60-90% of all illness. Since you do not want your beauty to be marred, see what God's Word has to say about these deadly emotional traps.

1. Anger

Anger takes many forms: envy, intolerance, criticism, revenge, hatred, rebellion, jealousy, and unforgiveness. Many of these plus other forms of anger are mentioned in Ephesians 4:31: "Let all bitterness and indignation and wrath (passion, rage, bad temper) and resentment (anger, animosity) and quarreling (brawling, clamor, contention) and slander (evil speaking, abusive or blasphemous language) be banished from you, with all malice (spite, ill will, or baseness of any kind)." God commands you not to be controlled by these carnal emotions which flow from your OSN because He wants you to be happy and beautiful. Look at yourself in the mirror when you are angry and see how your beauty is blemished.

A wife controlled by Jesus Christ is a crowning joy to her husband, but when she is controlled by anger, her presence can be torture: "It is better to dwell in a corner of the housetop [on the flat oriental roof, exposed to all kinds of weather] than in a house shared with a nagging, quarrelsome, and faultfinding woman. It is better to dwell in a desert land than with a contentious woman and vexation" (Proverbs 21:9, 19).

Are you aware that one form of torture is the continual dropping of water on one's head? The Bible suggests that an angry woman is like this hellish torment. "The contentions of a wife are as a continual dropping [of water through a chink in the roof]. A continual dripping on a day of violent showers and a contentious woman are alike" (Proverbs 19:13; 27:15).

God needs to give a command only once for it to be important. The fact that He refers frequently to the repugnance of an angry woman should warn you of the seriousness of anger. God does not want you to miss the point.

Anger has a way of multiplying and reproducing itself in the lives of your husband and children. "The north wind brings forth rain; so does a backbiting tongue bring forth an angry countenance. It is better to dwell in the corner of the housetop than to share a house with a disagreeing, quarrelsome, and scolding woman" (Proverbs 25:23-24). Could outbursts of anger from your family be caused by your own, perhaps unconscious, bad humor? Your family can reflect your moods, attitudes, and aspirations.

The usual cause of anger is identified by the ugly word "selfishness." When you are angry, it is usually because you feel that your rights have been violated. Or you want something done for you that has not been done, or you do not want something done that has been done. You can excuse and justify your weaknesses and even indulge in vengeful, bitter feelings, but the motivation is still selfishness.

Recognize the symptoms listed above as evidences that you are controlled by the OSN, confess them as sin and trust Christ to change you.

2. Fear

Fear is a trap that is as damaging to your beauty and health as anger. No kind of cosmetic will cover the self-consciousness, doubts, and fears reflected on your face. Fear may be displayed through anxiety, doubt, timidity, indecision, superstition, withdrawal, loneliness, overaggression, worry, feelings of inferiority, cowardice, hesitance, depression, haughtiness, or shyness.

What causes fear? It may be caused by a conscience that is guilty because of sin. Adam and Eve's first sin—partaking of the forbidden fruit—brought fear. "They heard the sound of the Lord God walking in the garden in the cool of the day, and Adam and his wife hid themselves from the presence of the Lord God among the trees of the garden. But the Lord God called to Adam, and said to him, 'Where are you?' He said, 'I heard the sound of You [walking] in the garden, and I was afraid, because I was naked; and I hid myself' " (Genesis 3:8-10). Sin caused them to hide, fearing the presence of the Lord, whereas before their sin they had enjoyed God's presence and fellowship.

Sin produces fear from which you try to escape either physically or mentally. "The wicked flee when no man pursues them, but the [uncompromisingly] righteous are bold as a lion" (Proverbs 28:1). You do not have to prove or justify yourself if you are not guilty. You need not be afraid if you are innocent. "There is no fear in love—dread does not exist; but full-grown (complete, perfect) love turns fear out of doors and expels every trace of terror! For fear brings with it the thought of punishment, and [so] he who is afraid has not reached the full maturity of love—is not yet grown into love's complete perfection. And, beloved, if our consciences (our hearts) do not accuse us—if they do not make us feel guilty and condemn us—we have confidence (complete assurance and boldness) before God" (1 John 4:18; 3:21).

If you have feelings of guilt, perhaps you *are* guilty. Compare your actions with God's Word in order to determine your true condition. If God's Word reveals your guilt, confess your sin and thank Jesus Christ for paying the penalty for it when He died for you on the cross. The Father forgives and forgets your sin because of Christ's work for you. "As far as the east is from the west, so far has He removed our transgressions from us" (Psalm 103:12). Do not look back or remember the sin again. Let it be a closed case.

Because of Christ's work on the cross for you, you may be free from the burden of a guilt complex. If you are guilty, confess your sin and accept Christ's forgiveness. Should the thought of your confessed sin enter your mind again, simply thank God that He has forgiven you and move on.

Fear may also come from not knowing or not believing God's Word. Peter's lack of faith in Christ caused him terror: "In the fourth watch [between three and six o'clock] of the night, Jesus came to them, walking on the sea. And when the disciples saw Him walking on the sea, they were terrified, and said, 'It is a ghost!' And they screamed out with fright. But instantly He spoke to them, saying, 'Take courage! I AM; stop being afraid!' And Peter answered Him, 'Lord, if it is You, command me to come to You on the water.' He said, 'Come!' So Peter got out of the boat and walked on the water, and he came to Jesus; but when he perceived and felt the strong wind, he was frightened, and as he began to sink, he cried out, 'Lord, save me [from death]!' Instantly Jesus reached out His hand and caught and held him, saying to him, 'O you of little faith, why did you doubt?' " (Matthew 14:25-31)

At first, Peter did not recognize Jesus and was terrified. When you do not recognize His power to work out solutions to problems in the world, you can become terrified too. Then Peter's trust in Christ enabled him to begin walking to meet Christ on the water. But the strong wind whipped up the sea and frightened Peter into doubting Christ's sufficiency for him.

Is this not what happens to you? When the problems or anticipated problems of life threaten, you begin to fear for yourself and your loved ones. You fear that you'll have to face demands you aren't strong enough to meet. And it is true that apart from Christ you can do nothing (John 15:5). Yet you can say with Paul, "I have strength for all things in Christ who empowers me—I am ready for anything and equal to anything through Him who infuses inner strength into me [that is, I am self-sufficient in Christ's sufficiency]" (Philippians 4:13).

Jesus Christ commands us not to fear and promises to give us victory regardless of the situation. "Fear not [there is nothing to fear] for I am with you; do not look around you in terror and be dismayed, for I am your God. I will strengthen and harden you [to difficulties]; yes, I will help you; yes, I will hold you up and retain you with My victorious right hand of rightness and justice" (Isaiah 41:10).

Christ lovingly reminds us of our heavenly Father's watchful care. "Are not two little sparrows sold for a penny? And yet not one of them will fall to the ground without your Father's leave and notice. But even the very hairs of your head are all numbered. Fear not, then; you are of more value than many sparrows" (Matthew 10:29-31).

Recognize the deadly trap of fear set for you by Satan. Claim Psalm 27:1: "The Lord is my light and my salvation; whom shall I fear or dread? The Lord is the refuge and stronghold of my life; of whom shall I be afraid?"

3. Depression

The final deadly trap that can ruin your beauty is mental depression. The increased sale of tranquilizers and antidepressants indicates that depression is a major problem in today's society.

Depression can be caused by an abnormal physical or spiritual condition. You can be depressed because of improper balance in your body chemistry or because of other physical malfunctions. If depressed, first consult a doctor to determine if the source of your depression is physical. If so, you can still be controlled by the Holy Spirit.

A violation of God's principles can also cause depression. Living by God's principles produces an abundant life but violating these principles results in a defeated existence. "Your ways and your doings have brought these things down upon you; this is your calamity and doom; surely it is bitter, for surely it reaches your very heart" (Jeremiah 4:18). The Lord reminded Cain of this principle just before he murdered his brother Abel. "The Lord said to Cain, 'Why are you angry? And why do you look sad and dejected? If you do well, will you not be accepted? And if you do not do well, sin crouches at your door; its desire is for you, and you must master it' " (Genesis 4:6-7).

Depression can be an advanced stage of anger or fear that you've allowed to go unchecked in your life. We have already established that anger and fear are basically selfishness. Selfishness, when indulged, may take the form of self-pity. Self-pity is very subtle. Often we try to justify it by thinking, "I didn't deserve such treatment," or "How unappreciative my husband is after all I've done for him." Depression, the price you pay for self-pity, is not worth the sick satisfaction it gives.

You can avoid depression by focusing your thoughts on your position in Christ rather than on conditions around you. "If then you have been raised with Christ [to a new life, thus sharing His resurrection from the dead], aim at and seek the [rich, eternal treasures] that are above, where Christ is seated at the right hand of God. And set your minds and keep them set on what is above—the higher things—not on the things that are on the earth. For [as far as this world is concerned] you have died, and your [new, real] life is hid with Christ in God" (Colossians 3:1-3).

Your position in union with Christ is the basis of all your spiritual life and growth. This position was established for eternity when you received Jesus Christ as your personal Saviour. "Therefore if any person is (ingrafted) in Christ, the Messiah, he is (a new creature altogether,) a new creation" (2 Corinthians 5:17).

At the moment of your salvation, you obtained a permanent relationship with God which guarantees, among other things, that you will live with God forever. All your sins were paid for by Christ; you have the life of Christ (eternal life), and you share the righteousness and destiny of Christ. In other words, you are the beneficiary of an inheritance as an heir of God and joint heir with Christ. Concentrating on your privileged status in Christ is like drawing on a million dollars that a benefactor has deposited in your bank account. Concentrating on unpleasant conditions is like living in poverty, unaware of those available riches.

The principle of focusing on your position in Christ can

also be illustrated in the following way. A roomful of women will have their minds on various details of life. One will be thinking about her neighbor's hair-style or dress. Another will be thinking about a point of conversation. But when a celebrity walks in, all the women will focus their attention on the celebrity. Our lives and attention are to be focused on the Celebrity Jesus Christ and our position in Him. Then, the details of life will fall into place, and we will begin to enjoy the inheritance that is already ours.

One beautiful thing about being God's child is that if you fall, you do not have to remain under the control of the OSN which disfigures you. You can escape Satan's traps with their marring effects. "They may come to their senses [and] escape out of the snare of the devil, having been held captive by him [henceforth] to do His [God's] will" (2 Timothy 2:26). You will escape if you follow these steps: (1) face your anger, fear, or self-pity as sin; (2) confess your attitude or action as sin (1 John 1:9); (3) accept Christ's forgiveness based on His work on the cross for you; and (4) trust Him to make the necessary changes in your life.

10
How to Handle Problems and Trials

Certain problems are common to each of us and it will be helpful to know what God's Word has to say about our response to them. As you apply God's solutions to the various situations, your spiritual beauty will blossom.

What principles do I apply when I make mistakes? "A man who refuses to admit his mistakes can never be successful. But if he confesses and forsakes them, he gets another chance" (Proverbs 28:13, LB). Admit your mistakes; do not try to excuse yourself.

Millie reaped great dividends when she applied this principle. In the midst of a hurried afternoon of juggling children's schedules and activities, she accidently locked her keys in the car. Since her husband Ralph, busy at work, had the only other key, she had to call him late in the day. He had not been sympathetic to her blunders before and didn't sound very happy this time when she phoned him.

"I'm sorry for the inconvenience this will cause you after such a hard day's work," Millie told him. "We'll wait here for you until you can come get us."

When Ralph arrived, he seemed to be pleased with his wife's sweet dependency on him. Instead of fussing at her, he rewarded her by taking the family out to dinner.

Don't be disappointed if your husband does not respond positively to your mistakes as quickly as Ralph did. You may have to patiently and lovingly win back your man's approval over a period of time. If so, you can be comforted by the fact that God forgives you immediately even if your loved one has not yet learned to. Your peace will come from knowing you are living according to God's will through His Word.

What about the mistakes your husband makes? "Love forgets mistakes; nagging about them parts the best of friends" (Proverbs 17:9, LB).

His mistakes will not be corrected by mistaken behavior on your part. "Don't repay evil for evil. Wait for the Lord to handle the matter" (Proverbs 20:22, LB).

How should you respond to criticism from your husband? "Don't refuse to accept criticism; get all the help you can" (Proverbs 23:12, LB). "The man who is often reproved but refuses to accept criticism will suddenly be broken and never have another chance" (Proverbs 29:1, LB). Take your husband's criticism as a reminder from the Lord to investigate your actions and make the proper adjustments. Remember God holds him responsible for his household, and may be using him to correct mistakes in your home.

Proverbs 25:12 (LB) tells us, "It is a badge of honor to accept valid criticism." Sometimes you may receive criticism that you feel is not valid. However, if you maintain a sweet, gentle spirit by drawing upon Christ's power within you, God will use even invalid criticism to develop your inner spiritual qualities.

How should you deal with contention and strife? Be sure to come to terms quickly with your husband when there is any discord between you. "Come to terms quickly with your accuser while you are on the way traveling with him" (Matthew 5:25). Don't let hurt feelings stand in the way of your making the first move to correct an unpleasant situation.

I had the opportunity to apply this principle shortly after learning it. My busy schedule was keeping me from my household responsibilities. DeWitt pointed this out to me one morning at breakfast after asking me when I was going to mend the pants he had given me weeks earlier.

I realized I was not as good a wife as I wanted to be and felt hurt. I let the Holy Spirit act as the anesthetist for my pain and managed to respond correctly with, "I'm sorry I didn't mend them earlier, DeWitt. Thanks for helping me get my priorities straight."

Since this was a new response on my part, he was as shocked as I was to hear it. After a moment of silence, he said, "Oh, that's all right. I was just feeling grouchy this morning and took it out on you."

You see, he reacted kindly because I had responded properly and promptly rather than attempting to justify or excuse my actions.

Contention or strife is easiest dealt with before it gets out of control. "The beginning of strife is as when water first trickles [from a crack in a dam]; therefore stop contention before it becomes worse and quarreling breaks out" (Proverbs 17:14). When fighting is allowed to continue, strong walls are built up that are difficult to remove. "It is harder to win back the friendship of an offended brother than to capture a fortified city. His anger shuts you out like iron bars" (Proverbs 18:19, LB).

What about unkind remarks your husband makes to you or about you? First, realize that he may be teasing you, not knowing how he is hurting you by what he considers an innocent comment. You owe it to him and yourself to tell him how you feel about what he says. He is not a mind reader; you cannot understand each other without communication.

Choose a time when your relationship is good and your husband seems to be in an understanding mood. Be sure your words and attitude are loving and in no way violate other principles (trying to get him to change or making him feel guilty). "Rather, let our lives lovingly express truth in all things—speaking truly, dealing truly, living truly. Enfolded in love, let us grow up in every way and in all things into Him, who is the Head [even] Christ, the Messiah, the Anointed One" (Ephesians 4:15).

Remember, acting in love does not mean you are to be a doormat or have an apathetic or passive attitude. You may express love in many ways. You may express it forcefully but never with a condemning or martyr-like attitude. You should also be realistic. If you adopt an absurd, overly sweet reaction to your husband's indiscretions, you'll place yourself on a pedestal where your husband can't reach you and love you and have a normal and real relationship with you.

It might not fit your personality, but one woman I know communicates her feelings to her husband through exaggerated words and actions. When her husband says something she doesn't like, she playfully sticks out her tongue or lower lip at him. When he ignores her, she says in mock self-pity something like, "I'm going out to eat green worms till I die. Then you'll be sorry!" Through such antics, she lets her husband know how she feels without getting angry. Her husband knows she has spunk and is fascinated by her.

If your husband does not refrain from unkind comments after you have expressed your feelings, you can apply the principle in Proverbs 10:12 (LB): "Hatred stirs old quarrels, but love overlooks insults." If you trust Christ to give you a forgiving attitude, He will build strong character in you.

What should your response be to sinful mental attitudes (pride, jealousy, bitterness, vindictiveness, implacability, guilt complex, hatred, worry, anger, and fear) in the lives of others, especially your husband? As always, God has an answer. "Answer not a [self-confident] fool according to his folly, lest you also be like him" (Proverbs 26:4). Folly here is referring to sins of mental attitude.

If your husband is controlled by a sinful attitude such as bitterness and you become involved emotionally with his problem, you too can be overcome by carnal emotions. Your involvement should be limited and nonemotional. If you are not caught up in the emotion, God will be able to deal directly with your husband, convicting or disciplining him as necessary. Any animosity your husband expresses will be between him and God. "Beloved, never avenge yourselves, but leave the way open for [God's] wrath; for it is written, 'Vengeance is Mine, I will repay (requite), says the Lord'" (Romans 12:19).

If a response is necessary, it should be quiet and filled with love. "A soft answer turns away wrath; but grievous words stir up anger" (Proverbs 15:1). This is the only response that will be effective and reap the desired results. "By long forbearing and calmness of spirit a judge or ruler is persuaded, and soft speech breaks down the most bonelike resistance" (Proverbs 25:15).

Perhaps you say, "My husband is so gross in his attitudes and actions that I cannot respect and reverence him as Ephesians 5:33 commands. What do I do about obeying this command?" The Christian life is a life of faith (trusting Christ to be who and what He claims). (See Hebrews 11:1, 6.) You can be sure that what God tells you to do, He is willing to perform through you. If you follow the principle of reverencing and responding to your husband by faith, your actions will demonstrate love, respect, and reverence even though you do not feel those emotions. God is faithful and will, according to your need, reward your obedience to His commands.

Many times we women get hurt unnecessarily because we don't understand our men. Do not consider your husband's unpleasant actions or attitudes a personal attack on you. Realize that business, physical, or emotional pressures may be causing his reactions. Remember, it is God's job to deal with him concerning his problem, not yours. Help him by sympathizing rather than adding to his problems by pouting, fussing, or whatever you do destructively when you are hurt or offended.

Many women have said, "My husband does not admire and praise me as he does others. How can I get him to?" "It is not good to eat much honey, so for men to seek glory, their own glory, causes suffering and is not glory" (Proverbs 25: 27). If you seek or demand your husband's praise, you'll cause trouble and hurt feelings.

You will attain praise and glory by focusing on Jesus Christ, His Word, and His will for your life. As you are occupied with Christ, He will provide you with praise and honor. "Prize wisdom highly and exalt her, and she will exalt and promote you; she will bring you to honor when you embrace her" (Proverbs 4:8). "Let not mercy and kindness [shutting out all hatred and selfishness], and truth [shutting out all deliberate hypocrisy or falsehood] forsake you. Bind them about your neck; write them upon the tablet of your heart; so shall you find favor, good understanding and high esteem in the sight [or judgment] of God and man" (Proverbs 3:3-4). As God's Word fills and controls your heart, you will gain the praise of your man. Wait for it; do not demand it.

How should you respond to praise from your husband or others? "The purity of silver and gold can be tested in a crucible, but a man is tested by his reaction to men's praise" (Proverbs 27:21, LB). You will not have a problem of pride if you are aware that you are simply a vessel God uses to do His good work. The most gracious way to respond to a compliment or praise is with a simple "thank you," reflecting a grateful heart.

Comparing yourself with others or fearing that others will not accept you as you are will always create problems. Do not spoil your beauty by getting your eyes on other people— allowing them to govern your attitudes, actions, and responses. "When they measure themselves with themselves and compare themselves with one another, they are without understanding and behave unwisely" (2 Corinthians 10:12). It is easy to think, "If I were like Sue, my husband would like me better." It never helps to try to copy another's dress, mannerisms, or personality. Your husband chose you because you were the one he preferred. You can pick up beauty hints or learn rules of etiquette from others, but do not try to be a carbon copy of another woman.

The fear of not being accepted is described in Proverbs 29: 25: "The fear of man brings a snare, but whoever leans on, trusts, and puts his confidence in the Lord is safe and set on high." This fear is not from the Lord, "For God did not give us a spirit of timidity—of cowardice, of craven and cringing and fawning fear—but [He has given us a spirit] of power and of love and of calm and well-balanced mind and discipline and self-control" (2 Timothy 1:7).

Being overly concerned about others' reactions to your husband's behavior can create problems between the two of you. You can know if you are overly concerned if you find yourself correcting your husband, seeking to clarify his actions or comments by further explanation, or apologizing for his behavior. He will take your comments as an indication that you do not trust his ability to handle a situation or make a favorable impression on others. He'll feel that you are not accepting him as he is and are attempting to be a "go-between" in his relationships with others. And he will be *right*.

If your husband has not made himself clear or has been

misunderstood, let him work out the problem. Only then will he gain self-confidence and improve his ability to communicate clearly and interact with others. It is your responsibility to encourage and comfort him, not to mother him, correct him, or improve him. You can avoid needless frustration and tension if you ask yourself, "Am I assuming responsibility that is not mine as his wife?" Many frustrations and tensions come when you assume responsibility which is not yours.

No matter what may be causing you unrest, disharmony, or confusion, God has set forth a principle in His Word through which you can gain harmony and peace. Ask yourself, "Can the problem that is causing distress be corrected or removed?" Even as you oil a squeaky door, so you can set a disorderly house in order. Correct the problem if possible. Otherwise trust God to use it to mold you into His image. He promises, "When a man's ways please the Lord, He makes even his enemies to be at peace with him" (Proverbs 16:7).

Your inner beauty will be apparent if you learn to take even small irritations in stride and allow Christ to use them to make you a lovelier person. One day, June was in a big hurry and spilled milk in the back seat of the car. Instead of panicking or getting angry, she asked God what He wanted to teach her through this irritation. He immediately reminded her that she needed to slow down. When she shared this thought with her husband, he said, "You're beautiful on the inside and the outside!"

Accepting God's Complete Provision Through Faith

Faith is another word for believing what God says in His Word even though you have no visible proof. The Christian life is a life of faith (2 Corinthians 5:7). You take many steps by faith: you receive Christ by faith; you are forgiven of your sins by faith; and you are controlled by the Holy Spirit by faith. Yet the results are not based on the amount of faith you have but on the object of your faith—Jesus Christ.

God wants you to enjoy, through faith, His complete provision for your daily needs. And it is wonderful to know that at the moment you received Christ, you received, potentially, all He could give you to meet those needs: "Blessed be the God and Father of our Lord Jesus Christ, who has blessed us with every spiritual blessing in the heavenly places in Christ" (Ephesians 1:3, NASB).

You are not to seek some ecstatic new experience. All you have to do is discover what is already yours in Christ through the Word and apply it by faith (see Colossians 2:3).

Any decision you make must *always* be based on the solid, unchangeable facts of God's Word rather than on how you feel. Moods and emotions come and go, but God's Word never changes. Sometimes your feelings motivate and encourage you, but other times they pull you down. So you see, your feelings should never be the basis for your actions. Your decisions must be based on facts about God and what He has done for you. A life of faith in Christ will not always be easy, but it is the only life that offers incorruptible beauty.

God taught Moses that by faith he could obey anything God said (see Exodus 4:2-4). The Lord asked Moses, "What do you have there in your hand?"

Moses replied, "A shepherd's rod."

"Throw it down on the ground," the Lord told him.

Moses' rod was familiar and useful to him as a shepherd. He had no reason to cast it before God except in obedience to God. Moses trusted and obeyed God on the basis of God's word alone, not because the request seemed sensible to Moses. Once Moses obeyed and dropped his rod, it became a serpent and Moses ran from it.

Then the Lord said to Moses, "Grab it by the tail!"

Moses could have responded with, "But what about the head, Lord? I'm frightened!" Instead, Moses again trusted God and when he did, the serpent became a rod in his hand. When we fulfill our responsibility by obeying and trusting the Lord, we can be confident that He will work out each detail of a situation for our benefit. Moses' rod was returned to him, but the serpent (representing any harmful ingredient) was removed.

Do you hesitate to surrender some facet of your life to the Lord as Moses hesitated to obey the Lord and drop his rod? Could it be that you are unwilling to totally trust the Lord with your husband, children, career, possessions? You, too, can accept and experience God's complete provision for you, through faith, by surrendering each area of your life to Christ, knowing that if He returns it to you, it will be purified and safe for your enjoyment. When you surrender areas of your life to Him, you do not lose anything; you gain fulfillment. You *can* trust Him!

Another way you can accept God's complete provision for you through faith is by thanking God for *everything* in your life. "Thank [God] in everything—no matter what the circumstances may be, be thankful and give thanks; for this is the will of God for you [who are] in Christ Jesus [the Revealer and Mediator of that will]" (1 Thessalonians 5:18). Thanking God for everything in your life shows that you believe God's Word. He says that even though everything in our lives is not good, He will work out all things for our good as we trust Him (see Romans 8:28).

Is this concept new to you? I had learned that I should give thanks in all things, but I had not applied this principle in my life. I was in the habit of thanking God for those things in my life that I knew were good and I could understand, but I had never thanked Him for the unpleasant situations. Finally, I decided to give thanks in all situations.

One morning my decision was tested severely. A heavy ice storm had covered the Atlanta area when DeWitt left for work. Later in the morning, his office called to see if he were coming in. I told them he had left about two hours before. The gentleman replied, "Since it only takes him about 30 minutes to drive to work, I guess he's had an accident on the icy expressway."

At that point, I had the choice of trusting and thanking God or giving way to hysterical fear. Knowing that God loved DeWitt more than I did, that He is sovereign, and that He promises not to allow anything to happen to His children without working it out to their benefit, I said, "Thank You, Lord, for whatever situation DeWitt is in."

God honored my obedience to His Word by giving me peace. "Peace I leave with you; My [own] peace I now give and bequeath to you. Not as the world gives do I give to you. Do not let your heart be troubled, neither let it be afraid— stop allowing yourselves to be agitated and disturbed; and do not permit yourselves to be fearful and intimidated and cowardly and unsettled" (John 14:27). The peace God gave me did not hinge on DeWitt's circumstances. As it turned out, DeWitt was delayed because of other accidents, not his own.

Apply this principle of giving thanks in all situations, especially to minor incidents in your daily life such as dropping an egg on your freshly waxed floor, an inconvenient telephone call, or an unappreciative husband. As you learn to be thankful in the small problems in your life, it will be natural to be thankful for larger trials and crises. Of course, you can rejoice only when you focus on Jesus Christ's sovereignty and His ability to work everything out to your good. Because of His sufficiency, you live above your circumstances instead of under them and life takes on a new, wonderful dimension. With a thankful heart, you will experience real joy, realizing that God will allow nothing to happen in your life that He can't work out for your benefit.

You see, joy does not depend on circumstances but on your

relationship and fellowship with God, as we've mentioned. If you choose to react to circumstances and people around you, you will be happy when your circumstances and other people are pleasant but sad when they are unpleasant. In other words, reacting to conditions around you produces an unstable existence.

As you reflect Jesus Christ, you can have peace and stability whether or not you get the dress you want or have to live with a grouchy husband. Accept the victory Christ promises you in John 16:33: "I have told you these things so that in Me you may have perfect peace and confidence. In the world you have tribulation and trials and distress and frustration; but be of good cheer—take courage, be confident, certain, undaunted —for I have overcome the world—I have deprived it of power to harm, have conquered it [for you]."

Do realize, however, that as Christ controls your life, He will not assume responsibilities He has assigned to you. For example, He will not do such things as make decisions for you or open your mouth in order for you to witness. But He will be your power once you make a decision and, in faith, act on it. When I first understood that Christ desired to live in and through me (see Galatians 2:20), I excitedly shared His desire with my three-year-old son. "Isn't it good news, Ken, that we can trust Christ to live through us rather than trying to do it ourselves?"

"Yes," he answered. "That's good."

Later, when I told him to pick up his toys he said, "Let Jesus do it. I don't have to."

I reminded him that Jesus would live His life through him by using his arms and legs to pick up toys.

Ken said, "Oh, is that how it works?"

Christ will not make your decisions for you but expects you to make them on the basis of His Word. Then He is your Power for carrying them out.

11

Completing the Picture

Real, fadeless inner beauty is created by Jesus Christ, the divine artist at work in you. Your inner self (the living canvas) becomes radiantly beautiful under His workmanship. Your body (the picture frame) complements or enhances the picture. Both the canvas and frame must be attractive if people are to enjoy the painting. An unattractive or inappropriate frame can detract from a good picture. A wisely chosen frame will add that extra touch that can make even an ordinary picture look beautiful.

It should encourage you to know that both your body or picture frame and your inner self or canvas are precious to God. "And the very God of peace sanctify you wholly; and I pray God your whole *spirit* and *soul* and *body* be preserved blameless unto the coming of our Lord Jesus Christ" (1 Thessalonians 5:23, KJV). If God considers your body to be important, you should too.

Try to make your body as attractive a part of the whole picture as possible. People form ideas about the "real you" by the outward clues you furnish. They accept you on the basis

126

of your own self-appraisal—often expressed in your grooming.

Since everything you do and are and even the way you look reflects on your Saviour as well as yourself, it is doubly important that you be well-groomed. "So then . . . whatever you may do, do all for the honor and glory of God" (1 Corinthians 10:31).

Your grooming should reflect self-respect and self-esteem. When you are not well-groomed, it is as if you are saying, "I consider myself unworthy of care. I don't think I'm valuable enough to spend time on." Yet when you remember that God considers your body important, that your looks reflect on your Saviour, and that you are a child of God, purchased by the blood of Jesus Christ, you can't help but rejoice and realize that you are a person of worth.

In fact you are a temple: "Do you not know that your body is the temple—the very sanctuary—of the Holy Spirit who lives within you, whom you have received [as a Gift] from God? You are not your own. You were bought for a price—purchased with a preciousness and paid for, made His own. So then honor God and bring glory to Him in your body" (1 Corinthians 6:19-20). Your body is a palace where Royalty lives! You will want it to be glorious and beautiful, shining and polished, to honor the King of kings. The psalmist expressed the desire "that our daughters may be as cornerstones, polished after the similitude of a palace" (Psalm 144:12, KJV).

There are those who say good grooming is worldly, that you are not spiritual when you are well groomed. These people often take the verse in 1 Peter 3:3 (KJV) as their basis and say you should not care for your hair, wear jewelry, or dress attractively. "Whose adorning let it not be that outward adorning of plaiting the hair, and of wearing of gold, or of putting on of apparel." Such people always stop in their reasoning before they finish the verse or they would have to conclude that we are not to put on clothing!

Man (OSN) is always trying to *do* something to make himself spiritual, whereas his spirituality is determined by whether or not Christ is controlling his life. A dowdy or "odd ball" appearance limits your effectiveness for Christ, but a pleasing, socially acceptable appearance gives you a wider witness for Christ. Good grooming is looking your best for Him, not drawing attention to yourself. Your overall appearance should be the best you can accomplish within your budget and should be in keeping with your role and position.

Your *role as a wife* involves developing a relationship with your husband that will bring joy to both of you. A *career* would involve spending time updating your skills so you could be successful in your field. In the same way, your *identity as a woman* requires you to spend time making and keeping yourself attractive. Of course you should not spend all your time, thought, and money on your appearance, but you will need to take some time to make yourself as lovely as possible: "sugar and spice and everything nice," as the old rhyme goes.

Sugar and Spice through Good Grooming

1. Cleanliness

One of the most important ways to be lovely is to be sure your body is as clean as possible. It has been said that "cleanliness is next to godliness." Reverence for God should produce reverence for your body. Bathing daily will help you stay clean and sweet-smelling all day and will help you feel dainty and feminine. Of course, your freshness will last only if you use a good deodorant to control unpleasant body odors.

Choose your favorite fragrance as a delightful finishing touch to your daily bath routine. When Ruth was preparing to win her husband-to-be, Naomi told her to "wash and anoint yourself therefore, and put on your best clothes and go" (Ruth 3:3).

2. Diet

Are you aware that what goes inside shows up on the outside? It is important to provide a healthy body for Jesus Christ to live in. And it requires self-discipline. If you want to maintain a healthy weight, you must prepare wholesome, nourishing, well-balanced meals for yourself and your family. If you have gained a few extra pounds, it is important to your health, your self-image, and your husband to lose them. But do consult a doctor before trying any severe reducing diet.

You can take sensible precautions against an over intake of calories by cutting down on between-meal snacks, heavy pastries, and rich desserts. You do not have to stop eating. Just train your taste buds to enjoy nonfattening, nourishing foods. Generally speaking, when you eat moderate portions of nourishing food, your weight will not fluctuate much. Find out how many calories you need to maintain your correct weight and eat accordingly.

3. Exercise

If you don't get enough exercise, you will feel sluggish, gain weight, and/or get flabby. Be sure you get exercise each day, outdoors if possible. If it is necessary for you to do some calisthenics, you might enjoy them more if you do them with a TV exercise program. However you do them, you will find that they move your blood, limber you up, and give you a firm, trim figure and more enthusiasm for life.

4. Rest

An active wife and mother also needs time to rest and relax. If you have small children, you may be able to rest only while they are taking naps. Regardless of when you do it, take time to relax and do not feel guilty about it. Jesus told His disciples to "come away by yourselves . . . and rest awhile" (Mark 6: 31, NASB). If the Son of God saw the need for relaxing, you should. It will help you stay fresh and alert through the evening when your husband and older children are home. Their day may be coming to a close but yours may last until late at night.

5. *Makeup*

Proper complexion care and makeup aids are important in achieving and maintaining a lovely complexion. Most cosmetic studios or large department stores have skin-care and makeup analysts to serve you without charge. Make use of their free service. They will give you tips on how to apply makeup for the most natural look. Remember that when makeup is skillfully applied, others will be aware of your loveliness, not your cosmetics.

Watch yourself in a mirror to see if you have any distracting facial mannerisms when you talk. Or ask a friend if she has noticed any. Do you chew or lick your lips? Do you grit your teeth or move your jaws from side to side? Make a conscious effort to correct such mannerisms.

6. *Hair*

A lovely face should be framed with a halo of beauty—your hair. A woman's hair is a symbol of her femininity. One of the ways your femininity contrasts with your husband's masculinity is through the care, style, and length of your hair. "Does not (experience, common sense, reason and) the native sense of propriety itself teach that for a man to wear long hair is a dishonor (humiliating and degrading) to him, but if a woman has long hair, it is her ornament and glory? For her hair is given to her for a covering" (1 Corinthians 11:14-15). Tousled, unkempt, and unattractive hair does not glorify God or add to your femininity.

For your hair to look as attractive as possible, it is necessary to brush, shampoo, and set it regularly. First, however, empty your piggy bank and get a professional haircut or, if you prefer long hair, a trim to get rid of split, dry ends.

The style of your hair should enhance the shape of your face. Consider current styles but do not choose one just because it is fashionable. After experimenting with your hair or trying on wigs or getting the help of a professional, pick a style that is best for you.

7. Hands

Nothing expresses the inner you more completely than your hands. Dry, shiny hands suggest that you are getting old. Red, chapped hands prove you wash dishes and floors but don't care about the aftereffects. Ragged nails and cuticles reveal that you are a nervous chewer. Dirty nails suggest that you are not completely clean.

Since neglected hands and nails definitely spoil the overall sugar and spice effect you want to project, keep your hands clean and soft and your nails shaped and clean. This will not take too much time if you keep hand lotion, an emery board, and a pair of rubber gloves (for dirty work or washing) ready.

Then be sure you do not spoil the effect of lovely hands by restless, nervous, fidgety actions. Nervous practices such as twisting your handkerchief or ring, gesturing, rubbing or stroking your chin, chewing your nails, or cracking your knuckles will mar your charm. Practice holding your hands in a graceful, relaxed position while sitting, standing, or talking.

8. Clothes

Carefully chosen clothes add the final touches to your feminine appearance. Clothing can create an illusion of a well-proportioned figure. You can accentuate your good points and camouflage your bad points through the use of line, color, fabric, and pattern to make yourself look taller, shorter, fuller, or thinner. You can get specific instructions on how to complement your individual figure at the larger department stores' modeling and fashion shows or through books or magazine articles.

The wise woman, as described in Proverbs 31, dresses well: "Her clothing is of linen, pure white and fine, and of purple [such as that of which the clothing of the priests and the hallowed cloths of the temple are made]" (Proverbs 31:22). It is better to choose a few well-made, fashionable dresses than many poorly-made garments. Trust Christ to guide you in choosing your wardrobe, and you will be amazed at the bargains you can find. Remember, though, that a bargain is not a bargain unless you need it. You can make your wardrobe appear larger than it is if you buy a few basic garments that you can vary through the use of scarves, belts, jewelry, vests, or mixing and matching.

And you can add to your wardrobe inexpensively by sewing. "She seeks out the wool and flax and works with willing hands to develop it" (Proverbs 31:13). If you do not know how to sew, you may be able to get instructions reasonably at a sewing center or in an adult education class at a local high school, college, or YMCA. You can get ideas for sewing by browsing in the more fashionable dress shops and noticing the trim, material, color combinations, and styles in use. Even looking through Sears', Ward's, or other catalogs will help you make your sewing look both professional and fashionable. The Lord tells you to ask Him for wisdom. He'll help you express your own personality through your dress.

Your clothing, like your hair, expresses your femininity in contrast to your husband's masculinity. God gives strict orders about a woman not wearing men's clothes and vice versa. "The woman shall not wear that which pertains to a man, neither shall a man put on a woman's garment; for all that do so are an abomination to the Lord your God" (Deuteronomy 22:5). This does not mean a woman cannot wear slacks, but slacks or pants outfits should be feminine. Unisex clothing does not glorify God. God wants a man's dress to be masculine and the woman's dress to be feminine, according to the culture's standards.

Yes, you will want to choose styles that flatter your figure and pick colors that enhance your skin tone. But be sure your husband approves of your clothing. You will please God when you dress in a way that pleases your husband.

9. Posture

No matter how well-groomed and daintily dressed you are, you will ruin the whole effect if you slump, hunch, or swagger. Practice standing, walking, and sitting gracefully. Stand tall, chest high. Keep your feet together when you sit or walk by keeping your feet parallel and your knees together.

These points about hair, hands, figure, dress, and posture may seem troublesome and time-consuming but as they become part of your outlook and routine, you'll find they are not a burden. Increasing your feminine charm will be worth all the time and effort you must take.

Everything Nice through Domestic Tranquility

Your sugar and spice appearance should be matched by "everything nice" around you. In other words, you want a setting of a tranquil, orderly household. That will mean planning, organization, and self-discipline on your part. If you feel you can't handle a home and family in an orderly manner, ask God's help. Since you are His child, you can go directly to Him in Jesus' name. "Let us then fearlessly and confidently and boldly draw near to the throne of grace—the throne of God's unmerited favor [to us sinners]; that we may receive mercy [for our failures] and find grace to help in good time for every need—appropriate help and well-timed help, coming just when we need it" (Hebrews 4:16).

God is orderly and wants you to have a peaceful life. "For He . . . is not a God of confusion and disorder but of peace and order. . . . But all things should be done with regard to decency and propriety and in an orderly fashion" (1 Corinthians 14:33, 40).

Jesus Christ promises to help us use our time wisely when we trust Him. "Reverence for God adds hours to each day; so how can the wicked expect a long, good life? I, Wisdom, will make the hours of your day more profitable and the years of your life more fruitful" (Proverbs 10:27; 9:11, LB).

When we are not organized and purposeful in our living, Christ is dishonored. "Look carefully then how you walk! Live purposefully and worthily and accurately, not as the unwise and witless, but as wise—sensible, intelligent people; making the very most of the time—buying up each opportunity—because the days are evil. Therefore do not be vague and thoughtless and foolish, but understanding and firmly grasping what the will of the Lord is" (Ephesians 5:15-17).

Design a plan by which you can accomplish your responsibilities. Then look to God for help. "We should make plans—counting on God to direct us" (Proverbs 16:9, LB). Keep in mind your priorities: (1) personal relationship with Jesus Christ, (2) husband, (3) children, (4) personal grooming and rest, (5) household responsibilities, (6) outside ministry. Before you schedule your daily activities, the following outline might be helpful in keeping your priorities in order:

1. Time with the Lord (studying His Word and prayer)
2. Meals, dishes, housework
3. Washing, ironing, grooming
4. Time with the family
5. Time to rest and relax
6. Individual hobbies, interests, and activities.

Start by making a list of the jobs you have to do. Then work out a reasonable schedule for getting them done. You may have to cut out some TV, unnecessary shopping, or long phone conversations. You may have to learn to say no to some good activities that are not essential. But if you know what your priorities are, you will not sacrifice the best for something that is merely good. You owe your husband your best, whether it's your attention, appearance, or providing a tranquil household.

Learn to make wise use of your time by carrying a book, or handwork such as sewing or writing, with you when you must wait in the car, at the doctor's office, or when you watch TV with the family. Save steps by placing items that go to the basement near the basement door. Make one trip at the end of the day rather than several during the day unless you need the exercise. Make good use of your time by having a long telephone cord on your kitchen phone so you can cook, clean your kitchen, sew, or iron while visiting with friends or making necessary calls. You can do some housework while listening to Bible study tapes that help you to grow spiritually.

Take the necessary time to train your children to care for their rooms, clothing, toys, and personal appearance. It may be easier to do their work yourself at first, but once your children are properly trained, their help will save you time. Besides, part of your job is to train your children to be self-reliant. You should not be doing things that the children can do for themselves.

Plan ahead and your life will not be regulated by the unexpected. Again, the wise woman of Proverbs 31 is a good example: "She fears not the snow for her family, for all her household are doubly clothed in scarlet" (v. 21). Her life was not regulated by disaster (snow). Sunday morning did not find her scurrying around ironing her son's pants. She foresaw his need and planned ahead.

Yes, you should plan and be organized but not inflexible. "We can make our plans, but the final outcome is in God's hands. Commit your work to the Lord, then it will succeed" (Proverbs 16:1, 3, LB).

Among your many responsibilities is that of buying and preparing food that pleases your husband. "She is like the merchant ships loaded with foodstuffs, she brings her household's food from a far [country]. She rises while yet it is night and gets spiritual food for her household and assigns her maids their tasks" (Proverbs 31:14-15).

It is well to rise early in the morning to fix your husband a good breakfast. Christ will help you enjoy cooking—even early in the morning—if you ask His help.

Discovering new and different ways to serve food can be fun. "Variety is the spice of cooking." Avoid preparing the same thing each week by adding new dishes that friends recommend or that look good in your cookbook. If your husband's likes are limited, try to fix the foods he likes as tastily as possible. But do serve a new dish occasionally for your children's sake.

When you prepare a favorite dish of the family, try doubling the recipe and freezing half for unexpected company or a quick family meal.

God has given you the exciting, fulfilling, rewarding ministry of being a wife and mother. You have inexhaustible opportunities for supporting and complementing your husband's ministry as well as for training your children. Their lives will, in turn, affect hundreds of other lives. No other person can have the influence on your family that you have as wife and mother.

Your role includes a wide range of skills. As God enables you to develop these, you will find that in your own home you are teacher, nurse, interior decorator, manager, dietitian, seamstress, purchasing agent, counselor, consultant, photographer, you name it. What greater challenge could any woman want?

Your ministry in your home can be an exciting creative adventure. And most important, if Christ is controlling your life, you are serving Him as you care for your family. You are serving Christ just as certainly as the evangelist who is seeing hundreds saved each day. God's plan for you as a woman will completely satisfy you if you allow Him to direct every area of your life.

Everything Nice Via Emotional Stability

"Everything nice" includes your emotional stability. One way to maintain balance is to develop a sense of humor. Do not take yourself too seriously. "A happy heart is a good medicine and a cheerful mind works healing. . . . He who has a glad heart has a continual feast [regardless of circumstances]" (Proverbs 17:22; 15:15). You are to your family atmosphere what a thermostat is to the temperature of your home. If you are relaxed about life, your home will have a relaxed atmosphere. If you can laugh with your children and husband (especially at his jokes) and laugh at yourself, your home will be a happier place for your family.

Avoid crying to get attention or your own way. Your husband may give in to you in frustration, not knowing any other way to handle you, but you will have damaged your relationship. Crying to get your way is like demanding love but getting sympathy; you get results but not the ones you really want.

There will be times when household tasks, mistakes in household management, routine child care problems, and decisions regarding meals may cause you to become discouraged. Do not bother your husband with these routine problems. Instead, go to Jesus Christ for your strength and guidance. "Work hard and cheerfully at all you do, just as though you were working for the Lord and not merely for your masters, remembering that it is the Lord Christ who is going to pay you, giving you your full portion of all He owns. He is the One you are really working for" (Colossians 3:23-24, LB). These words, addressed to servants, apply to anyone who has tasks to perform.

One of the qualities of an emotionally stable person is a grateful attitude. This attitude is developed through Christ's controlling your life as you regularly study God's Word. "And let the peace (soul harmony which comes) from Christ rule (act as umpire continually) in your hearts—deciding and settling with finality all questions that arise in your minds— [in that peaceful state] to which [as members of Christ's] one body you were also called [to live]. And be thankful—appreciative, giving praise to God always" (Colossians 3:15). You can be grateful for every person in your life as you realize that Christ promises to work out all things (or use any persons) for your benefit as you trust Him. If you have a grateful spirit, your husband will enjoy your company and be more likely to become the husband you need.

Let gratitude be your response when your husband gives you a gift. Remember that your husband and his thoughtfulness are more important than what he gives you. Therefore accept anything he gives you with a joyful spirit and sincere appreciation.

Never reject a gift he buys for you. If he should buy you a size 16 dress when you wear a size 10, let him go with you to exchange it for something he likes. If you cannot stand the perfume he gave you, use a little more than necessary when he is around, and he may suggest that you stop wearing it. Let it be his decision, not yours.

What if he does not give you gifts? Examine your past actions to see if you have violated any of the principles we have established. If not, you simply may be married to a man who does not enjoy shopping (by the way, few men do). Accept him as he is!

You foster an "everything nice" atmosphere when you understand how to ask your husband for what you want or need. Do not hint. Men are usually so preoccupied with their activities that they do not catch subtle hints. Then their wives feel hurt, thinking their men do not love them. Avoid trying to convince him of your need in order to get your way. He may feel trapped and rebel. Demanding your way does not work either because in demanding you are usurping his authority, and he feels offended by your actions. Instead, ask for things with a simple "May I, please?" or "Will you, please?" When you use this simple straightforward method, you will find him more willing to grant your requests. Of course you should be careful not to ask for things he cannot afford.

Try not to be shaken if your husband should have a reaction known as "Pandora's Box" when you start applying God's principles to your marriage. He may have suppressed hateful feelings toward you through the years, fearing that if he vented his real feelings his marriage would break up. Now that he knows you accept him as he is, all these suppressed feelings may suddenly come rolling out. If this happens, ask Jesus Christ to relieve any hurt feelings you may have. Do not argue with your husband, but encourage him to share his feelings with you. When he is through expressing his hostilities, he will, hopefully, be free of bitterness toward you and be free to begin loving and cherishing you.

Everything Nice through Your Individuality

Many women are afraid that they will lose their individuality if they subject themselves to their husbands. Yet the wise woman of Proverbs 31:10-31 is definitely an individual though she obviously seeks to please her husband: "She will do him good and not evil all the days of her life" (v. 12, KJV). Paradoxically, only when you submit to God—in any area—do you know the fullest freedom and power: "If the Son therefore shall make you free, ye shall be free indeed" (John 8:36, KJV). See also John 14:21, 23; Galatians 3:28, and Galatians 5:1.

Having cared for your responsibilities as wife and mother, you can find ways to express your individuality: thinking up new menus or recipes, decorating your home, planting a vegetable garden, planning a surprise party for some family member, inventing some new activity to keep your youngsters occupied or some new means of settling their quarrels, following the stock market, writing letters or stories, painting pictures. Whatever your interests are, develop and enjoy them, even put them to work in your home. Because your husband knows he is first in your life, he will be glad for you to express your individuality in your home and even have outside interests and hobbies—so long as they don't take too much of your time and attention.

Your husband will actually be comforted and fascinated by the fact that you are an individual in your own right. "Strength and dignity are her clothing and her position is strong and secure" (Proverbs 31:25). Your husband can be relaxed if his business detains him, knowing that you have plenty of interests to keep you busy in his absence. He may enjoy your dependency but not the yoke of your helplessness.

As you work at making yourself and your home attractive, your husband should be able to say, "There are many fine women in the world, but you are the best of them all!" (Proverbs 31:29, LB)

12

Physical Fulfillment

God has provided a way in which you and your husband can experience and express the deep, intimate relationship He intends for you. That way is through your sexual union. God's plans are so perfect that there is no area in which He has not made total provision for your needs whether they be spiritual, psychological, sociological, or physical. He is interested in your complete personal fulfillment.

Sex—God's Idea

We see that sex is God's idea because it was part of His plan in making the man and woman. "And the Lord God said, 'It is not good that the man should be alone; I will make him an help meet for him.' So God created man in His own image, in the image of God created He him; male and female created He them. And God said unto them, 'Be fruitful, and multiply, and replenish the earth, and subdue it' " (Genesis 2:18; 1:27-28, KJV).

After God made Eve from Adam's rib, He gave Eve to Adam and said, "Man shall . . . become united and cleave to his wife and they shall become one flesh" (Genesis 2:24). Thus, God instituted the marriage relationship. The marriage of Adam and Eve set a pattern for mankind so that the human race could be perpetuated in maximum freedom, protection, and happiness.

God designed the sexual union of husband and wife to be an expression of love for each other. This union is described by the word "cleave" meaning "to be joined"—a sexual relationship. God meant this relationship to be a fulfilling, enjoyable part of the lives of husband and wife. The Song of Solomon, as well as many other Scriptures, describes in vivid language the physical delight experienced in the union of the bodies of married lovers (Song of Solomon 6:1-10 and 7:1-9).

Since Scripture teaches that, for married people, an effective Christian life and good sexual adjustment go together, you should strive for the latter as well as the former, remembering that "marriage is honorable in all and the bed undefiled" (Hebrews 13:4, KJV).

The physical union of you and your husband should be good and satisfying because it is an expression of your inner oneness. Being one in the soul means that your mind is filled with thoughts of your husband, you commit your will to doing his will, and no one will ever take his place in your affections. The sexual union, then, becomes more than just a physical act since it portrays a much deeper soul relationship between you two. Without unity of soul, the sex act is an improper union of bodies and is not fulfilling.

Distortions or Abuses of God's Plan for Sex

Distortions or abuses of sex come from the OSN or from Satan himself. Satan is a master distorter and counterfeiter of God's wonderful provision for mankind. Distortions will emphasize the body or sex without the soul relationship or vice versa. Since God has designed a complete, satisfying relationship for you, He has set certain boundaries or prohibitions. This is because He loves you and desires you to be happy.

God has prohibited adultery (sex with someone other than your mate), for example, because it destroys your soul oneness with your husband. The fact that adultery can destroy you as a person is revealed in Proverbs 6:32 (KJV): "But whoso committeth adultery with a woman lacketh understanding; he that doeth it destroyeth his own soul."

God also says that adultery affects the body: "Any other sin which a man commits is one outside the body, but he who commits sexual immorality, sins against his own body" (1 Corinthians 6:18). Adultery can affect your body by causing you not to be able to function properly, sexually, and by taking away full enjoyment with your mate. In a woman, promiscuous sex can lead to nymphomania (insatiable sexual desire)or frigidity (lack of or decreased sexual desire). The corresponding effects in a man would be satyriasis and impotence.

Furthermore, both man and woman can become laden with guilt as a result of adultery. God warns us not to distort or misuse sex but to enjoy it within the boundaries He has set.

Another abuse of sex is the practice of autoeroticism or masturbation. God says in 1 Corinthians 7:4 that married people are not to arouse their own bodies sexually. This is the right of your husband only. "The wife does not have the right to do as she pleases with her own body; the husband has his right to it. In the same way the husband does not have the right to do as he pleases with his own body; the wife has her right to it" (1 Corinthians 7:4, WMS). Since masturbation is a means of self-gratification only, it is an abuse of God's plan for sex to be an expression of love between husband and wife. Also, the sexual drive should never control you, but it may if you become engrossed in self-gratification.

When you enjoy sex according to God's plan, distortions

and abuses of sex such as masturbation, homosexuality, lesbianism, bestiality, wife-swapping, pornographic activity, sensitivity concepts, and polygamy will not be part of your life.

Sex itself is not wrong; but the misuse or distortion of it is. "Marriage is honorable in all and the bed undefiled, but whoremongers and adulterers God will judge" (Hebrews 13:4, KJV).

Sex can be compared to another of God's good gifts—food. "For everything God has created is good, and nothing is to be thrown away or refused if it is received with thanksgiving. For it is hallowed and consecrated by the Word of God and by prayer" (1 Timothy 4:4-5). Food, when eaten in the proper proportions and balance, provides health and pleasure. When you violate these boundaries, you can become a glutton. The sun, also God's gift, provides warmth and light but can cause pain when you overexpose tender skin to its rays. The Bible gives a balanced, healthy view of sex. God does not hide the details; neither does He glamorize or glorify the wrong use of sex. God's information is complete and perfect!

If you have been involved in immoral sex practices, remember that Jesus Christ paid for that sin also. Confess your immorality as sin, accept Christ's forgiveness, and move on to a life of fulfillment in His will. As Jesus said to the adulterous woman, "Go and sin no more" (John 8:11, LB).

Marital Delights
God gives beautiful, positive instruction in Proverbs 5:15, 18-19 (LB) on how a couple's sexual needs are to be fulfilled through union in marriage. "Drink from your own well, my son—be faithful and true to your wife. Let your manhood be a blessing; rejoice in the wife of your youth. Let her charms and tender embrace satisfy you. Let her love alone fill you with delight." The wife is referred to symbolically in these passages as a well and in some translations as a

"cistern," as "fresh running water," and as a "fountain." The beautiful parallel is between a person's thirst being satisfied by drinking cool, fresh water and a couple's sexual thirst being satisfied by regular sexual union in marriage.

Notice that God says to "rejoice in the wife of your youth." The sexual relationship is to provide you with great pleasure. The wife is described as tender, charming, loving, and *satisfying*. You are to concentrate on making your sex life a satisfying, fulfilling experience for your husband. Otherwise, how can he "let her love alone fill [him] with delight"? A woman should have great freedom and joy in satisfying her husband's sexual desires and needs.

You must realize that your husband needs the freedom to initiate whatever sexual actions he desires, knowing you will respond lovingly. You can be relaxed in the knowledge that it is God's will for you to meet his needs enthusiastically. As you do, your mutual fulfillment and enjoyment will grow.

Mutual sexual fulfillment has not always been a reality in Karen and Fred's life, but it is now. While growing up, Karen had not been taught God's plan for sex. As a result, she had many hang-ups. The sordid stories she had heard about marital sex caused her to think of her role in physical relations as an obligation or duty she dreaded. The books Karen read on sex did not release her from her warped ideas. Almost any techniques of love-play and sexual arousal left Karen burdened with a deep sense of guilt. She felt that to enjoy such activities would be perversion.

After hearing the lectures on which this book is based, Karen got a different perspective. Her eyes sparkled as she said, "I had no idea God had so much to say in His Word about sex. The Scriptures you mentioned showed me that sex is God's idea, not man's. It's designed to give pleasure to both my husband and me. I've learned to relax totally and enjoy the genuine desire we now have for each other."

Solving Sex Problems

You must look for the source of sex problems if you want to find permanent solutions. Since sex in marriage is an expression of the inner oneness of two people, it follows that problems can relate to any facet of either mate's life. Problems can be spiritual or personality maladjustments, or they may simply stem from not understanding each other.

Realizing how you and your husband differ sexually may help correct some sexual problems. Generally, the man has a more aggressive, stronger sex drive than the woman. This is understandable since God created the man to be the leader. Knowing this, you can simply respond to his sexual leadership and expect complete satisfaction for both of you rather than being "turned off" by his aggressiveness and need. Furthermore, a man is usually stimulated sexually by sight but a woman normally is not. Should your husband watch you undress for bed, he may become sufficiently aroused to be ready for intercourse while you are simply ready for bed.

Also, a man and woman may differ in sexual response after an argument. Your husband's way of saying, "Please forgive me and let me show you how much I love you" may be to have sexual union. But you may prefer to be reassured of his love with tender words and caresses before you are ready for sex. Furthermore, sex can serve as a tranquilizer for your husband, enabling him to relax and go to sleep. When you are tired, the last thing you may want is sex.

It may help you, too, to realize that your husband may feel his masculinity is tied in with his ability to satisfy your sexual needs. If your husband is unsure of his masculinity, he may attempt to cover up or compensate for real or imagined deficiencies. He may display his insecurity by refusing sexual relations or accelerating sexual behavior. He may be afraid that you will reject his sexual advances, or he may fear that he won't be able to adequately meet your needs.

You can help your husband avoid these fears if you realize that he has a greater physical-emotional challenge in the sexual union than you do. The success of the act depends on his ability to obtain and maintain a strong erection. Support him by displaying your confidence in his sexual ability through word and deed. You may convey this by embracing him eagerly, kissing him warmly, or by sighing in appreciation at the right time. Your actions should give the unmistakable impression that you can hardly wait to enjoy union with him.

You may be thinking, "Am I to pretend?" Since you know God planned this relationship for your enjoyment, pretending should never be necessary. Therefore, look at it as if you are simply anticipating your own sexual excitement and communicate this eagerness to your husband. The most effective way to give your husband pleasure is to let him know you care about him and desire to have intercourse with him.

What if your husband is not interested in you sexually? Remember, a beautiful sex relationship does not start when you go to bed. The relationship is an expression of lives lived in an atmosphere of love. Ask Christ to show you if you have unintentionally been critical, cutting, sarcastic, or jealous, or if you have implied that your husband's sexual abilities are inferior or inadequate for you.

Joan tried to get her husband to go for a medical checkup, feeling his inability to have union with her was a physical problem. Finally, her husband handed her an article he had clipped from the paper. It said in essence that a man does not find a woman appealing, sexually, if she is constantly bickering or has attacked his masculinity by not allowing him to be the leader, provider, and protector in his home. As you trust Jesus Christ for your attitudes and actions and fulfill your role as wife, your inner "oneness" will be right and sexual problems will begin to disappear.

Never be guilty of using sex as a weapon, whether to punish your husband or to get something from him. When you withhold your body for such reasons, you are making a prostitute of yourself because you are selling your body to your husband in exchange for something you want. Paul tells us: "For the wife does not have [exclusive] authority and control over her own body, but the husband [has his rights]. . . . Do not refuse and deprive and defraud each other" (1 Corinthians 7:4-5). If you place a price tag on your sexual relationship, your husband may feel the price is too high and go shopping for a better bargain.

Sexual problems can also result if either you or your husband has a warped idea of love, sex, or marriage because of childhood experiences. For instance, as a child you might have asked your mother the very normal question, "Where do babies come from?"

Your mother may have said, "Nice little girls don't ask such questions. When you get bigger you will learn about such things."

Because of her attitude, you may have concluded that there is something wrong about "where babies come from" and you did not question her any more about such things. You may have gotten the rest of your sexual education in an atmosphere of secrecy, causing you to feel sex was "dirty" rather than a beautiful, God-given expression of love. If your mother's attitude or an unfortunate childhood experience has been the root of your resentments and frigidity, renounce your wrong feelings about sex. Accept God's forgiveness and allow Him to give you a positive, healthy reaction to sex.

Sometimes a wife is not satisfied, sexually, because her husband doesn't understand her. Even though the greater percentage of sexual success is a result of your attitude, at least 20% depends on his education. Your husband may not be aware that a woman is not usually sexually aroused as quickly as a man and needs tender words and longer love play before she is ready to enjoy orgasm. If this is true in your marriage, guide your husband gently, showing him actions and expressions that please you. Then respond with enthusiasm.

When you respond to his efforts positively and with enthusiasm, he will be encouraged to make other efforts to please you. Let him know how much you enjoyed his efforts by telling him, "You were just wonderful tonight." If you did not reach a climax, you can still respond positively. A climax or orgasm is not always necessary for your sexual union to be a pleasing experience. You will discover, however, that as you wholeheartedly desire to satisfy your husband and respond positively to his actions, you will also have sexual satisfaction.

Should you ever take the initiative sexually? Yes. It is good for you to take the initiative at times. When you do, any fears your husband has that you may reject him sexually will be dispelled immediately. Also, he will likely be stimulated by the idea that you find him sexually desirable. Many times a man's impotence is overcome by being near his "turned-on" wife. He is made aware of his sexual ability and is encouraged to enjoy the sex act. However, do be careful not to become too aggressive in your sexual initiative.

As a result of your aggressiveness and sexual demands, your husband could be repulsed, feeling that he is not "the man in charge." Your sex life, as well as all other areas, must be balanced. When your husband's leadership in your home is not threatened, he will enjoy and be encouraged by your taking sexual initiative at times.

The wise woman plans ahead in order to meet her husband's sexual needs. Get the rest necessary in order to be alert, responsive, and available to your man. When you are tired or are not particularly interested in sexual union, trust

Jesus Christ to give you a new excitement and enthusiasm since it is His will for you both to receive pleasure and fulfillment through this union.

Let your schedule be flexible so that you will be available to meet your husband's needs at night, in the morning, or in the middle of the day.

Sense when your husband is interested in love-making. Don't be like the wife who finds all sorts of things to do before going to bed or reads *Good Housekeeping* in bed until her husband turns over and forgets the whole thing. True, you can't be a mind reader, but do be sensitive. Know your husband.

Prepare yourself to make love by thinking positive thoughts that would arouse you rather than cause you to be irritated. If you fulfill your role as a wife by accepting your husband as he is, admiring him, making him the center of your life, and responding to his leadership, provision, and protection of you, you will not need to be afraid of losing him to another woman. The basic reason for most unfaithfulness in marriage is emotional rather than sexual. Your husband's infidelity may be revenge for real or imaginary mistreatment. You should know more about his needs and wants than any other woman. By acting on this knowledge, you will tip the scales significantly in your favor.

Regardless of your sexual needs or problems, you can trust Jesus Christ to provide solutions. He promises to give wisdom to all who ask. "If you want to know what God wants you to do, ask Him, and He will gladly tell you, for He is always ready to give a bountiful supply of wisdom to all who ask Him; He will not resent it" (James 1:5, LB). He may provide this wisdom through His Word, the counsel of your pastor, a mature Christian, or through information received from a book. The heavenly Father is interested in your sexual life being totally fulfilling for both you and your husband. As you begin to understand your husband, you will become the wife he needs.

"Newness" in Marriage

Do not ever let it be said of your marriage that the "newness" has worn off or that life has become dull and routine. You can give new life to your marriage by saying or doing the unexpected. For instance, after you greet your husband with a kiss when he comes home from work, whisper in his ear, "I'm in the mood for love; how about now?" Of course you don't literally expect him to take you up on your suggestion since there may be children around and dinner to prepare. The thought, however, will stimulate him and remind him that he is desirable. This is just another way of saying, "I love you."

Some men want their wives to read dirty books or go to X-rated movies to see how they can add variety to their sex life. Show your husband you can provide variety and excitement without such "aids."

You can add freshness and variety to your marriage by making yourself beautiful, your bedroom irresistible, and your bed beautiful and comfortable. "She makes for herself coverlets, cushions, and rugs of tapestry" (Proverbs 31:22). Here are some suggestions you might use to gradually add "newness" to your marriage. Notice, I said gradually since your husband could be overwhelmed or even suspicious if you used all suggestions at once.

1. Keep your bed clean and sweet smelling. If your husband likes perfume, spray a little of his favorite on the pillows or sheets. Satin sheets and fur throws and pillows add a nice variety.

2. Use candlelight, soft light, or black light to produce a romantic atmosphere. Millie said her husband had never been the "candlelight type." However, when she introduced candle-

light to their bedroom, they both were thrilled with the effect.

3. The use of soft music can add a touch of newness to your sex life.

4. When circumstances permit, variety may be obtained by having sexual union in different rooms, perhaps in front of a glowing fireplace. Be responsive and be willing to have sexual union in a variety of positions.

5. When children are around, be sure you have privacy and a relaxed atmosphere. Lock your bedroom door if necessary.

6. Do not spoil the inviting scene you have created by appearing in curlers or face cream, and do use breath mints, spray, or mouthwash. A thing as simple as bad breath may keep your husband at a distance.

7. If possible, splurge on a new gown, and dress attractively for him, drawing his attention to your best features. Every woman has at least one good feature on which she can capitalize. It may be beautiful ankles, thighs, shoulders, neck, or breasts. *Make the most of what you have and don't fret about what you do not have.* Your most appealing outfit may be your "birthday suit." Never be embarrassed at being naked in front of your husband. Remember, your body belongs to him (1 Corinthians 7:4).

8. Keep your husband aware of your womanliness—the fact that you are an exciting woman and his lover, not just his children's mother. You can exhibit your stimulating, challenging womanhood through your creativity as you add spice and variety to your life. For instance, arrange for the children to spend a night or weekend with friends and have your husband's favorite meal by candlelight. Wear his favorite perfume, relax, and enjoy him.

Your bedroom should be the most beautiful room in your home since this is the room where you and your husband regularly display your love for each other. Always reserve this room for love—not for quarrels, though a Christian couple may well come to God on their knees in the bedroom to ask His forgiveness for sharp words and wrong attitudes.

You are glorifying Jesus Christ when you think and plan toward being a good sexual partner for your husband. You are reminded in 1 Corinthians 7:34, "The married woman has her cares [centered] in earthly affairs, how she may please her husband." When you make your sex life an exciting and satisfying part of your life, you will please your husband and, at the same time, you will be obedient to Christ's instructions to you.

If you do not fulfill your husband's sexual needs, you may be a stumbling block in his life and cause him to be led away from spiritual truths instead of toward God. "Do not refuse and deprive and defraud each other . . . lest Satan tempt you [to sin] through your lack of restraint of sexual desire" (1 Corinthians 7:5).

As you make sex an exciting and meaningful part of your lives, your husband will not be tempted to feel that he is "missing out" or that the "newness" of marriage has worn off. He will look forward to the sexual and emotional gratification he has with you.

In Conclusion

Your husband will be the happy man you want him to be when he feels that you accept him as he is, admire him for his masculinity, and put him first and foremost (after God) in your life. He will feel needed at home because he knows he is respected as the family leader, provider, and protector.

As you respond to your husband and fit into his plans according to God's order, you will see God perform the impossible in your marriage. When your husband is with you, he will feel complete and fulfilled, because you are his counterpart—giving him what he does not have alone.

This beautiful relationship between you is focused in a

sexual union where your love and affection are expressed, increased, and fortified. The sexual union makes possible a tender understanding, communion, and communication that cannot be expressed in language. As "one flesh" you are able to do together what neither of you can do alone.

When the principles set forth in this book become a part of your life, you will find fulfillment in your personal life and marriage. You will have a closer relationship to God, who ordained marriage. And you will discover that you are a real woman—the wife of a happy husband.

Epilogue

After I began applying the God-given truths in this book, my husband, DeWitt, asked me to give up teaching my weekly neighborhood Bible class to develop a course on the woman's role in marriage. Out of the lecture series came this book, first published in 1974.

After teaching the course for four years in Atlanta, and periodically conducting seminars elsewhere, I realized I was in danger of not following what I was teaching because of the time needed in my growing ministry. So God led me to place the "Happy Husband" series on audio and videotapes and I began concentrating on my relationships with Christ and DeWitt.

My home became and is presently the quarters for His Way Library—the means of retailing my teaching tools. With fewer speaking engagements there was room for more consecrated growth in the Lord and more time for writing. The sequel to this book, *The Beauty of Beholding God,* came into existence in 1982.

Our lives took a sharp turn about a year after this book was published. DeWitt attended a men's retreat and came home asking our sons to forgive him for not being the father he should have been. It was the first time we had seen him shed tears. At the retreat he had finally found salvation in Jesus Christ. Before, we thought that he was a Christian but just not completely yielded to God.

One year later, DeWitt and I went into full-time Christian work with Family Consultation Service, a ministry to the poor in the inner city of Atlanta. DeWitt built some 80 houses for the needy and I worked with family selection and community building. We also began a "crash" course in our relationship. I had to learn to relate to the new DeWitt, and we had to deal with problems that had been previously avoided. Sometimes I forgot that the same truths I had lived by for years still applied. Jesus was faithful to remind me of my mistakes. Happily, DeWitt and I find that our appreciation and love for each other grows daily. We have a closer unity than we ever believed possible.

In 1993 God dramatically moved us, DeWitt's mother, two of our sons and their families to north Georgia where our youngest son was already established. For 16 months, four generations lived under the same roof, until our middle son's house was built. Our oldest son has started a church in the area. We believe that God is allowing us to live out Malachi 4:5-6 that He used to call us to this area.

In 1994 I updated and refilmed my two video series, *You Can Be the Wife of a Happy Husband* and *A Wise Woman Honors God.* This last series is a synthesis of *You Can Be the Wife of a Happy Husband* and *The Beauty of Beholding God.* My speaking is usually in collaboration with groups that commit to study one or more of my series.

GALATIANS

EXPERIENCING THE
GRACE OF CHRIST

12 STUDIES WITH COMMENTARY
FOR INDIVIDUALS OR GROUPS

JOHN STOTT *BIBLE STUDIES*

JOHN STOTT

WITH DALE LARSEN AND SANDY LARSEN

An imprint of InterVarsity Press
Downers Grove, Illinois

InterVarsity Press
P.O. Box 1400
Downers Grove, IL 60515-1426
ivpress.com
email@ivpress.com

Inter-Varsity Press, England
36 Causton Street
London SW1P 4ST, England
ivpbooks.com
ivp@ivpbooks.com

InterVarsity Press® is the book-publishing division of InterVarsity Christian Fellowship/USA®, a movement of students and faculty active on campus at hundreds of universities, colleges, and schools of nursing in the United States of America, and a member movement of the International Fellowship of Evangelical Students. For information about local and regional activities, visit intervarsity.org.

Inter-Varsity Press, England, originated within the Inter-Varsity Fellowship, now the Universities and Colleges Christian Fellowship, a student movement connecting Christian Unions in universities and colleges throughout Great Britain, and a member movement of the International Fellowship of Evangelical Students. That historic association is maintained, and all senior IVP staff and committee members subscribe to the UCCF Basis of Faith. Website: www.uccf.org.uk.

All Scripture quotations, unless otherwise indicated, are taken from The Holy Bible, New International Version®, NIV®. Copyright © 1973, 1978, 1984, 2011 by Biblica, Inc.™ Used by permission of Zondervan. All rights reserved worldwide. www.zondervan.com. The "NIV" and "New International Version" are trademarks registered in the United States Patent and Trademark Office by Biblica, Inc.™

This study guide is based on and includes excerpts adapted from The Message of Galatians ©1968 by John R. W. Stott, originally published under the title Only One Way.

Cover design and image composite: Cindy Kiple
Interior design: Daniel van Loon
Images: wild flamingos abstract painting © work by Lisa Kling / Moment Collection / Getty Images

ISBN 978-0-8308-2173-0 (print)
ISBN 978-0-8308-5592-6 (digital)

Printed in the United States of America ∞

InterVarsity Press is committed to ecological stewardship and to the conservation of natural resources in all our operations. This book was printed using sustainably sourced paper.

P	25	24	23	22	21	20	19	18	17	16	15	14	13	12	11	10	9	8	7	6	5	4	3	2	1
Y	38	37	36	35	34	33	32	31	30	29	28	27	26	25	24	23	22	21	20

CONTENTS

INTRODUCING GALATIANS

Have you ever been led astray? Have you been convinced by a dynamic speaker or a persuasive book only to later find out that it was wrong?

We are most easily convinced when we are young or not well informed on a particular topic. The new Christians in Galatia were in just such a position when false teachers launched an attack on the gospel of grace and the authority of the apostle Paul.

GETTING TO KNOW THE GALATIANS

In the course of the thirty years or so that elapsed between his conversion outside Damascus and his imprisonment in Rome, the apostle Paul traveled widely through the empire as an ambassador of Jesus Christ. On his three famous missionary journeys he preached the gospel and planted churches in the provinces of Galatia, Asia, Macedonia (northern Greece), and Achaia (southern Greece). Moreover, his visits were followed by his letters, by which he helped supervise the churches he founded.

One of these letters, which many believe to be the earliest that he wrote (about AD 48 or 49), is the epistle to the Galatians. I believe "Galatia" is a reference to the four cities of Pisidian Antioch, Iconium, Lystra, and Derbe, which Paul evangelized during his first missionary journey. You can read about this in Acts 13 and 14.

A MESSAGE FOR US

The false teaching in Galatia centered on faith versus law. What is required of us to be Christians? Some were saying we must follow Old Testament law. Again and again Paul directs them back to Jesus Christ as the one who saves.

While the kinds of laws Christians today attempt to follow may differ, this is nonetheless an issue for us. We need to be reminded that we cannot save ourselves through righteous actions. Our only hope of salvation is in Jesus.

SUGGESTIONS FOR INDIVIDUAL STUDY

1. As you begin each study, pray that God will speak to you through his Word.

2. Read the introduction to the study and respond to the question that follows it. This is designed to help you get into the theme of the study.

3. The studies are written in an inductive format designed to help you discover for yourself what Scripture is saying. Each study deals with a particular passage so that you can really delve into the author's meaning in that context. Read and reread the passage to be studied. The questions are written using the language of the New International Version, so you may wish to use that version of the Bible. The New Revised Standard Version is also recommended.

4. Each study includes three types of questions. *Observation* questions ask about the basic facts: who, what, when, where, and how. *Interpretation* questions delve into the meaning of the passage. *Application* questions (also found in the "Apply" section) help you discover the implications of the text for growing in Christ. These three keys unlock the treasures of Scripture.

   Write your answers to the study questions in the spaces provided or in a personal journal. Writing can bring clarity and deeper understanding of yourself and of God's Word.

5. In the studies you will find some commentary notes designed to give help with complex verses by giving further biblical and cultural background and contextual information. The notes in the studies are not designed to answer the questions for you. They are to help you along as you learn to study the Bible for yourself. After you have worked through the questions and notes in the guide, you may want to read

the accompanying commentary by John Stott in the Bible Speaks Today series. This will give you more information about the text.

6. Move to the "Apply" section. These questions will help you connect the key biblical themes to your own life. Putting the application into practice is one of the keys to growing in Christ.

7. Use the guidelines in the "Pray" section to focus on God, thanking him for what you have learned and praying about the applications that have come to mind.

SUGGESTIONS FOR MEMBERS OF A GROUP STUDY

1. Come to the study prepared. Follow the suggestions for individual study mentioned above. You will find that careful preparation will greatly enrich your time spent in group discussion.

2. Be willing to participate in the discussion. The leader of your group will not be lecturing. Instead, she or he will be encouraging the members of the group to discuss what they have learned. The leader will be asking the questions that are found in this guide.

3. Stick to the topic being discussed. Your answers should be based on the verses that are the focus of the discussion and not on outside authorities such as commentaries or speakers. These studies focus on a particular passage of Scripture. Only rarely should you refer to other portions of the Bible. This allows for everyone to participate on equal ground and for in-depth study.

4. Be sensitive to the other members of the group. Listen attentively when they describe what they have learned. You may be surprised by their insights! Each question assumes a variety of answers. Many questions do not have "right" answers, particularly questions that aim at meaning or application. Instead the questions push us to explore the passage more thoroughly.

When possible, link what you say to the comments of others. Also be affirming whenever you can. This will encourage some of the more hesitant members of the group to participate.

5. Be careful not to dominate the discussion. We are sometimes so eager to express our thoughts that we leave too little opportunity for others to respond. By all means participate! But allow others to also.

6. Expect God to teach you through the passage being discussed and through the other members of the group. Pray that you will have an enjoyable and profitable time together but also that as a result of the study you will find ways that you can take action individually and/or as a group.

7. It will be helpful for groups to follow a few basic guidelines. These guidelines, which you may wish to adapt to your situation, should be read at the beginning of the first session.

   • Anything said in the group is considered confidential and will not be discussed outside the group unless specific permission is given to do so. We will provide time for each person present to talk if he or she feels comfortable doing so.

   • We will talk about ourselves and our own situations, avoiding conversation about other people.

   • We will listen attentively to each other.

   • We will be very cautious about giving advice.

8. If you are the group leader, you will find additional suggestions for you at the back of the guide.

FALSE TEACHERS AND FAITHLESS CHRISTIANS

GALATIANS 1:1-10

The devil disturbs the church as much by error as by evil. When he cannot entice Christian people into sin, he deceives them with false doctrine.

Reading Galatians 1, you may be surprised to see how the Galatian people have allowed themselves to be turned away from the true gospel by false teachers. Paul's reaction was one of astonishment. Yet this pattern of distorting the gospel continues today. Many evangelists have been similarly distressed to see how quickly, how readily, converts relax their hold of the gospel that they seemed to have so firmly embraced. It is, as Paul writes in Galatians 3:1, as if someone has cast a spell over them. By being aware of these dynamics we can keep ourselves from being led astray.

OPEN

How do you "test" the truth of what you hear from public figures, your pastor, and other Christian teachers?

STUDY

Read Galatians 1:1-5. Since Paul's visit to the Galatian cities, the churches he founded had been troubled by false teachers called Judaizers. The false teachers had launched a powerful attack on Paul's authority and gospel. They contradicted his gospel of justification by grace alone through faith alone, insisting that for salvation more than faith in Christ was needed. You had to be circumcised as well, they said, and keep all the law of Moses. Having undermined Paul's gospel, they proceeded to undermine his authority also. "Who is this fellow Paul, anyway?" they asked scornfully. "He certainly wasn't one of the twelve apostles of Jesus. Nor, so far as we know, has he received any authorization from anybody. He is just a self-appointed imposter."

1. What key themes emerge in verses 1-5 in response to the controversy with the false teachers?

2. How was it significant in light of the controversy for Paul to say he is an apostle "sent not from men nor by a man, but by Jesus Christ and God the Father"?

3. Create an outline of the gospel based on verses 1-5.

Summary: What the apostle has in fact done in these introductory verses of the epistle is to trace three stages of divine action for humanity's salvation. Stage 1 is the death of Christ for our sins to rescue us out of this present evil age. Stage 2 is the appointment of Paul as an apostle to bear witness to the Christ who died and rose again. Stage 3 is the gift to us who believe of the grace and peace that Christ won and Paul witnessed to. At each of these three stages the Father and the Son have acted or continue to act together. No wonder Paul ends his first paragraph with a doxology.

4. *Read Galatians 1:6-10.* In every other epistle, after greeting his readers, Paul goes on to pray for them or to praise and thank God. In contrast, what does he do in this letter?

5. The Greek word in verse 6 for "deserting" means "to transfer one's allegiance." It is used for soldiers in the army who revolt or desert and those who change sides in politics or philosophy. How is it appropriate for the Galatians as they are described here?

6. The false teachers were trying to "pervert" the gospel (v. 7) or, according to the Greek, to completely "reverse" the meaning of the gospel. Thus the Galatians were forsaking the gospel of grace for a gospel of works. Fill in this chart, contrasting these two ways of thinking as you understand them.

GRACE	WORKS

So the two chief characteristics of the false teachers are that they were troubling the church and changing the gospel. These two go together. You cannot touch the gospel and leave the church untouched, because the church is created and lives by the gospel. Indeed, the church's greatest troublemakers (now as then) are not those outside who oppose, ridicule, and persecute it but those inside who try to change the gospel.

7. How do you account for Paul's strong words in verses 8-9?

8. Verses 8 and 9 tell us that we are to judge the teacher by the gospel and not judge the gospel by them. Why is this distinction important?

9. Why does Paul add this "disclaimer" in verse 10?

10. The popular view is that there are many ways to God and that the gospel changes with the changing years. How could you argue against that using Paul's perspective in these verses?

Summary: How can we recognize the true gospel? First, it is the gospel of grace, of God's free and unmerited favor. Whenever teachers start exalting humanity, implying that we can contribute anything to our salvation by our own morality, religion, philosophy, or respectability, the gospel of grace is being corrupted. Second, the true gospel is the New Testament gospel. The norm by which all systems and opinions are to be tested is the gospel that the apostles preached and that is now recorded in the New Testament. Anyone who rejects the apostolic gospel is to be rejected.

APPLY

Who do you know who is being swayed by false teaching, and how can you help that person?

When are you likely to judge the gospel according to a teacher rather than judging the teacher by the gospel?

PRAY

Following Paul's example, list the steps in your life that led you to an understanding of the true gospel. Use this as a source of prayer and praise to God.

RADICAL CHANGE

GALATIANS 1:11-24

So far in his letter to the Galatians, Paul has explained that there is only one gospel, the criterion by which all human opinions are to be tested. Without doubt it is a very wonderful gospel. But where did Paul get it all from? Was it the product of his own fertile brain? Was it stale secondhand stuff with no original authority? Did he steal it from the other apostles in Jerusalem as the false teachers evidently maintained?

To prove that he received his gospel directly from Christ, Paul offers evidence from his own autobiography—his radically changed life.

OPEN

When someone you know undergoes a radical change, what kinds of questions does it raise for you?

STUDY

Read Galatians 1:11-17. Paul claims that his gospel, which is being called into question by the Judaizers and deserted by the Galatians, was neither an invention (as if his own brain had fabricated it) nor a tradition (as if the church had handed it down to him) but a revelation (for God had made it known to him). Paul dared to call the gospel he preached "my gospel," not because he had made it up but because it had been uniquely revealed to him.

1. What were the driving forces in Paul's life before his conversion?

2. What evidence is there that God was working in Paul's life even before his conversion to Christ?

3. What steps did Paul take to deliberately avoid human consultation about the gospel?

4. Why does Paul take care in countering the accusations that he got his gospel from someone else?

5. How does Paul's preconversion life add weight to his claim that his gospel came from God?

Summary: Having made the startling claim to a direct revelation from God without human means, Paul goes on to prove it from history, that is, from the facts of his own autobiography. Paul's situation before his conversion, at his conversion, and after his conversion show that he clearly got his gospel not from any human being but directly from God.

6. *Read Galatians 1:18-24.* How does Paul pile up additional evidence that he was not unduly influenced by the apostles or others?

7. At the beginning of his Christian life, Paul did not totally avoid other Christians, but he restricted his contacts. What did his caution accomplish in his life?

8. Paul had a direct revelation from God. How can you use the Scriptures, God's revelation to us, to exercise discernment and wisdom in whom you allow to influence you spiritually?

9. Given his reputation, how might Paul have expected the churches to respond to him as a supposed new believer?

10. What significance do you see in the fact that the Christians in Judea "praised God because of" Paul rather than praising Paul?

Summary: Before his conversion, Saul of Tarsus was a bigot and a fanatic, wholehearted in his devotion to Judaism and in his persecution of Christ and the church. A man in that mental and emotional state is in no mood to change his mind. No conditioned reflex or other psychological device could convert him. Only God could reach him—and God did!

APPLY

A startling change in a person's life can mean many different things. When has God made a radical change in your life that some people at first didn't understand?

Think of someone you know who has undergone a big change. How can you tell whether that change has been brought about by God or is the result of some human error or sin?

What are the biggest changes that knowing Christ has brought about in your life? Praise God for how he has worked and continues to work in you.

PRAY

What changes in your life would you still like the Lord to bring about? Pray for your will to be in cooperation with God's workings.

ONLY ONE GOSPEL

GALATIANS 2:1-10

Paul's detractors have plenty of successors in the Christian church today. It is fashionable in some quarters to talk about the "Pauline" gospel and the "Petrine" gospel and the "Johannine" gospel, as if they were quite different from one another.

But all this is mistaken.

The apostles of Jesus Christ do not contradict one another in the New Testament. Certainly there are differences in style between them because their inspiration did not obliterate their individual personality. There are also differences of emphasis because they were called to different spheres and preached or wrote to different audiences. But they complement one another.

OPEN

What aspects of the gospel sometimes seem contradictory to you, even if intellectually you know they are consistent?

STUDY

One of the ways in which some false teachers of Paul's day tried to undermine his authority was to hint that his gospel was different from Peter's and indeed from the views of all the other apostles in Jerusalem. They were trying to disrupt the unity of the apostolic circle.

To prove that his gospel was independent of the other apostles, Paul stressed that he paid only one visit to Jerusalem in fourteen years and that this lasted only fifteen days. To prove that his gospel was yet identical with theirs, he now stresses that when he paid a proper visit to Jerusalem, his gospel was endorsed and approved by them.

1. *Read Galatians 2:1-5.* In this passage, what points is Paul especially striving to get across?

2. Why was it wise for Paul to keep his meeting with the apostles private?

3. What is significant about the apostles' response to Titus?

4. How could Paul have been found to be "running his race in vain"?

5. Paul implies that giving in to the false teachers would mean a descent into slavery. In what senses could a Christian become a slave?

Summary: Paul saw the issue plainly. It was not just a question of circumcision and uncircumcision, of Gentile and Jewish customs. It was a matter of fundamental importance regarding the truth of the gospel, namely, of Christian freedom versus bondage. Acceptance before God depends entirely on God's grace in the death of Jesus Christ received by faith.

Read Galatians 2:6-10. What was the outcome of Paul's consultation with the Jerusalem apostles? Did they contradict Paul's gospel? Did they modify it, edit it, trim it, supplement it? No. Paul says, "They added nothing to my message" (v. 6). Further, they gave Paul "the right hand of fellowship" (v. 9). They recognized that they and Paul had been entrusted with the same gospel. The only difference between them was that they had been allocated different spheres in which to preach it.

6. What did the apostles in Jerusalem have to be convinced of in order to accept Paul's preaching?

7. The approval of Peter, James, and John was crucial to the case Paul was making in this letter. Then why does he apparently downplay their importance (v. 6)?

8. What distinction do the other apostles see in Paul's ministry (vv. 7-9)?

9. What significance do you find in the fact that the apostles accepted Paul's ministry when they saw the grace given to him (v. 9) rather than the persuasive gifts or intelligence or preaching abilities given to him?

10. What are some distorted versions of the gospel that you have heard?

11. How did you discover that these versions had altered the true gospel?

12. How would you answer someone who says that the gospel needs to be updated and revised in order to meet changing needs in changing times?

Summary: There is only one gospel, the apostolic faith, a recognizable body of doctrine taught by the apostles of Jesus Christ and preserved for us in the New Testament. If there is only one gospel in the New Testament, there is only one gospel for the church.

APPLY

Think of some Christian groups whose style grates on your nerves (for example, their music, preaching, dress, general approach, architecture, or worship). How does seeing that there is only one gospel help your acceptance of them?

Think of some Christian groups who choose to emphasize things you don't think are crucial (certain social concerns, doctrinal points, or lifestyle issues you consider gray areas). How does seeing that there is only one gospel affect your understanding of them?

PRAY

Thank God for your unity with other Christians. Pray that you will increasingly *feel* your unity as well as know about it.

FACING CONFLICT

GALATIANS 2:11-21

Without doubt it is one of the most tense and dramatic episodes in the New Testament. Here are Paul and Peter, two leading apostles of Jesus Christ, face-to-face in complete and open conflict. Both were Christian men, men of God, who knew what it was to be forgiven through Christ and to have received the Holy Spirit. Both were apostles of Jesus Christ, specially called, commissioned, and invested with authority by him.

Yet here is the apostle Paul opposing the apostle Peter to his face, contradicting him, rebuking him, condemning him, not because of Peter's teaching but because of his conduct. There is much for us to learn from this dramatic situation.

OPEN

When have you seen a conflict erupt between church leaders? What was it about, and how was it resolved (if it was)?

STUDY

1. *Read Galatians 2:11-13.* Describe the situation that concerns Paul.

2. Taking into account Paul's previous meeting with Peter, James, and John in Jerusalem (study 3), why would Paul have been especially incensed at Peter's behavior in Antioch?

Only a short while previously, as is recorded in Acts 10 and 11, Peter had been granted a direct, special revelation from God that Gentiles who believed must be welcomed into the Christian church. There is no suggestion in Galatians 2 that Peter had changed his mind. Why then did he withdraw from fellowship with Gentile believers in Antioch?

Paul's charge is that Peter and the others acted in insincerity and not from personal conviction. The Greek word for "insincerity" is the word from which we get the English word *hypocrisy*. Their withdrawal from table fellowship with Gentile believers was not prompted by any theological principle but by craven fear of a small pressure group.

3. What did Peter have to fear from the circumcision group?

4. Why do small pressure groups in the church arouse such fear in the majority and even in the leadership?

5. When have you given in to pressure and acted insincerely out of fear rather than from personal conviction?

Summary: The same Peter who had denied his Lord for fear of a servant girl (Mark 14:66-72) now denied him again for fear of the circumcision group. He still believed the gospel, but he failed to practice it. If Paul had not taken his stand against Peter that day, either the whole Christian church would have drifted into a Jewish backwater and stagnated or there would have been a permanent rift between Gentile and Jewish Christendom. Paul's outstanding courage on that occasion in resisting Peter preserved both the truth of the gospel and the international brotherhood and sisterhood of the church.

6. *Read Galatians 2:14-16.* What made this issue worth the danger of a public confrontation?

7. In some Christian fellowships believers hesitate to confront each other, and in others they confront each other too quickly. What are the spiritual dangers of each approach?

8. How would keeping in mind what Paul called "the truth of the gospel" (v. 14) have affected the situation you recalled in question 5?

Summary: Paul's opposition to Peter was just the kind of open, head-on collision that the church would seek at any price to avoid today. Paul acted as he did out of a deep concern for the very principle that Peter lacked. Notice the spiritual perception into the fundamental issue—that Peter and the others were not "walking straight" (literally, v. 14) according to the truth of the gospel. Paul is determined to defend and uphold the gospel at all costs, even at the expense of publicly humiliating a brother apostle.

Paul's critics argued like people still argue today: "If God justifies bad people, what is the point of being good? Can't we do as we like and live as we please?" But a person who is united to Christ is never the same person again. It is not just the person's standing before God that has changed; it is the person who has changed—radically, permanently changed. In one sense, we live this new life through faith in Christ. In another sense, it is not we who live it at all but Christ who lives it in us.

9. *Read Galatians 2:17-21.* Why would the gospel of God's grace bring down the accusation that "Christ promotes sin"?

10. Christians who are sure of their salvation can still be caught sinning. How does Paul deal with that uncomfortable fact?

11. Paul said that he no longer lives, but Christ lives in him (v. 20). How do you reconcile his words with the fact that Paul was still very much alive?

12. Why would Christ have "died for nothing" if righteousness could be gained through keeping the law (v. 21)?

Summary: If God does not require works of the law before he accepts people, how dare we impose a condition on them that he does not impose? If God has accepted them, how can we reject them?

APPLY

Many are the vocal pressure groups in the contemporary church. We must not be stampeded into submission to them out of fear. If they oppose the truth of the gospel, we must not hesitate to oppose them. When the issue before us is trivial, we must be as pliable as possible. But when the truth of the gospel is at stake, we must stand our ground.

What current pressures are you aware of—on yourself or within your Christian fellowship—to add conditions to the truth of the gospel?

What actions would help to keep accountability in light of those pressures?

PRAY

In what areas do you need to let Christ more fully live his life through you? Pray that you will live even more deeply "by faith in the Son of God."

FAITH AND WORKS

GALATIANS 3:1-14

Dear idiots" (J. B. Phillips) begins this section of Galatians. Paul sees the Galatians' turning away from the gospel as an act of spiritual treason (1:6) and folly. Indeed, so stupid was it that Paul wonders if some sorcerer "has bewitched" them. The Galatians knew perfectly well that the gospel is received by faith alone. How could they turn away?

OPEN

In what areas of life are you tempted to try to earn God's favor by your good actions?

STUDY

Throughout most of chapters 1 and 2 Paul has been stoutly defending the divine origin of his apostolic mission and message. Now he comes back to the Galatians and to their unfaithfulness to the gospel as a result of the corrupting influence of the false teachers. Having embraced the truth at the beginning (that sinners are justified by grace, in Christ, through faith), they have now adopted the view that circumcision and the works of the law are also necessary for justification. The essence of Paul's argument is that their new position is a contradiction of the gospel.

1. *Read Galatians 3:1-9.* What words and phrases reveal Paul's attitude toward the Galatians?

2. Twice Paul calls the Galatian Christians "foolish" (vv. 1, 3). In what senses is it foolish to add works to the gospel of Christ?

3. In artwork Christ is portrayed in many ways: teaching crowds, working alongside Joseph in the carpenter shop, praying in Gethsemane, welcoming children, walking on water. Why would Paul choose to focus on portraying Christ as crucified?

The gospel is not good advice to people but good news about Christ, not an invitation to us to do anything but a declaration of what God has done, not a demand but an offer. If the Galatians had grasped the gospel of Christ crucified, that on the cross Christ did everything necessary for our salvation, they would have realized that the only thing required of them was to receive the good news by faith. To add good works to the work of Christ was an offense to his finished work.

4. After beginning our Christian lives by faith, most of us at one time or other imitate the Galatians and fall into relying on our own efforts. Why do you think this happens?

5. To the Judaizers who were misleading the Galatian Christians, Abraham was a hero and patriarch. How does Paul turn the tables and use Abraham as an example of faith instead of law keeping?

6. What do we have in common with Abraham?

Summary: All this, the apostle says, the Galatians should have known. They should never have fallen under the spell of these false teachers. Indeed, they would not have done so if they had kept Christ crucified before their eyes. We, too, should learn to test every theory and teaching by the gospel of Christ crucified, especially as it is known to us from Scripture and from experience.

7. *Read Galatians 3:10-14.* The ugly words *curse* and *cursed* appear often in this passage. What justifies Paul's use of such language?

8. Why is there a curse hanging over those who try to rely on observing the law?

9. The "curse of the law" from which Christ redeemed us must be the curse resting on us for our disobedience (v. 10). And he redeemed us from it by "becoming a curse" himself. He voluntarily took our curse upon himself in order to deliver us from it. What does it mean to you that Christ became a curse for us?

10. What are some differences between law and faith?

11. In your own experience, what does it mean to "live by faith"?

12. What are some obstacles to living by faith?

Summary: No one can be justified before God by works of the law. It is quite true, as an axiom, that "the person who does these things will live by them" (v. 12). But nobody (except Jesus) has ever done them; therefore, nobody can live by them. The dreadful function of the law is to condemn, not to justify. Jesus Christ has done for us on the cross what we could not do for ourselves.

APPLY

Consider ways that you might have fallen into trying to please God or earn his favor by your own efforts. How does this passage encourage you to examine your heart?

Think of someone you know who is struggling with self-effort. How can you help restore that person to trust in Christ?

PRAY

Name all the ways you can think of that Jesus Christ has done for you what you could not do for yourself. Praise him for his sufficiency.

STUDY SIX

THE GIFT OF THE LAW

GALATIANS 3:15-29

Some try to go to Jesus without first meeting Moses. They want to skip the Old Testament, to inherit the promise of justification in Christ without the prior pain of condemnation by the law. We need the law to lift off the lid of our respectability and disclose what we are really like underneath—sinful, rebellious, guilty, under the judgment of God, and helpless to save ourselves. Not until the law has humbled us even to hell will we turn to the gospel to raise us to heaven.

There are some, however, who go to Moses and the law to be condemned and stay in this unhappy bondage. They are still living in the Old Testament. Their religion is a grievous yoke, hard to bear. They have never gone to Christ to be set free.

OPEN

Consider the above paragraph describing two responses to God's law. Which one tends to describe your life?

STUDY

1. *Read Galatians 3:15-22.* Trace the steps of Paul's argument that the introduction of law through Moses (the "mediator" of v. 19) does not supersede God's promise to Abraham.

The Greek word in verses 15 and 17 is translated "covenant," but it was in common use for a will. (See Hebrews 9:15-17, where the two ideas of a covenant and a will are also linked together.) The point Paul is making is that the wishes and promises that are expressed in a will are unalterable. Paul may be referring to ancient Greek law by which a will, once executed and ratified, could not be revoked or even modified. Or he may be saying that it cannot be altered or annulled by somebody else. God promised an inheritance to Abraham and his posterity. God's purpose was not just to give the land of Canaan to the Jews but to give salvation (a spiritual inheritance) to believers who are in Christ.

2. Why is a will an appropriate metaphor for the point Paul is making?

3. How is Christ foreshadowed in God's promise to Abraham?

4. God's promise to Abraham was made a very long time ago. How do modern-day Christians still participate in it?

5. Why must we choose between relying on the law and relying on the promise?

6. If God's law can't save anyone, why did God give it to humanity?

Summary: Paul is moving toward the conclusion that the Christian religion is the religion of Abraham and not of Moses, of promise and not of law, and that Christians are enjoying today the promise that God made to Abraham centuries ago. But in this passage, having contrasted these two kinds of religion, he shows the relation between them. After all, the God who gave the promise to Abraham and the God who gave the law to Moses are the same God!

Read Galatians 3:23-29. Paul uses two vivid similes in verses 23 and 24. The law expresses the will of God for his people, telling us what to do and what not to do, and warns us of the penalties of disobedience. But thank God, he never meant this oppression to be permanent. Its purpose was to shut us up in prison until Christ should set us free or to put us under tutors until Christ should make us God's children.

7. How does law lead us toward Christ?

8. What are some comparisons between being in prison and trying to earn God's favor by following his law?

9. How do people resist the "guardian" that is trying to lead them to Christ?

10. What difference does it make for you to see yourself as a child of God?

11. What difference does it make for you to see other Christians as children of God?

12. Differences of race, social standing, and gender obviously exist among Christians. What should be Christians' attitude toward these natural differences?

Summary: Paul has painted a vivid contrast between those who are "under the law" and those who are "in Christ," and everybody belongs to one category or the other. If we are "under the law," our religion is a bondage. But if we are "in Christ," we have been set free. Our religion is characterized by "promise" rather than by "law." We know ourselves related to God and to all God's other children in space, time, and eternity.

APPLY

Not until the law has arrested and imprisoned us will we pine for Christ to set us free. How did God's law lead you to Christ?

In what ways do you find yourself being drawn back under the bondage to law?

Where would you like to see oneness in Christ become more of a reality, and what can you do to help it happen?

PRAY

Praise God for how he faithfully keeps his promises. Pray that you will continually trust his promises.

CHILDREN OF GOD

GALATIANS 4:1-20

F ather, I would rather be your slave than your child."

Who among us would make such an odd request of our parents? Yet that was the folly of the Galatians, under the influence of their false teachers.

The way for us to avoid the Galatians' folly is to let God's Word keep telling us what we have and are in Christ. One of the great purposes of daily Bible reading, meditation, and prayer is just this, to get ourselves correctly orientated, to remember who and what we are.

OPEN

When and why have you had an especially strong awareness that you are a child of God?

STUDY

1. *Read Galatians 4:1-11.* What are the key images being used in this passage?

2. Legally, what does it mean to be an heir as a child (minor)?

Even in Old Testament days, before Christ came and when we were under the law, we were heirs—heirs of the promise that God made to Abraham. But we had not yet inherited the promise. We were like children during the years of their minority; our childhood was a form of bondage.

3. What are the differences between the way a slave on an estate and the child of the estate owner would relate to the master (owner)? (Think of differences in conversation together, physical bearing toward each other, attitude toward the estate, and how time in each other's presence is spent.) How does this parallel your relationship with God as his child?

4. What are the "elemental spiritual forces of the world" (v. 3) that used to hold us in slavery?

5. The term *Abba* (v. 6) is the term Jesus himself used to address God as "Father" when he prayed in Gethsemane (Mark 14:36). How should such intimate terminology affect our prayers?

6. How do you respond to the idea that you not only know God but are known by God (v. 9)? Do you find it comforting? unsettling? cheering?

Summary: The Christian life is the life of sons and daughters; it is not the life of slaves. It is freedom, not bondage. Of course, we are slaves of God, of Christ, and of one another. We belong to God, to Christ, and to one another, and we love to serve those to whom we belong. But this kind of service is freedom.

7. *Read Galatians 4:12-20.* In what sense(s) did Paul want the Galatians to become like him (v. 12)?

8. What was the contrast between how the Galatians had originally received Paul and how they now regarded him? Why?

9. How could Paul approve of their welcoming him "as if I were an angel of God, as if I were Christ Jesus himself" (v. 14)?

10. What was the contrast between what Paul and his companions wanted for the Galatians and what the false teachers wanted?

11. How does Paul share in the love and suffering of Christ for the Galatians?

12. Why do you think Paul has refused to give up on the Galatian church?

Summary: Paul appeals to the Galatians with immense tenderness. He longed for them to become like him in his Christian faith and life, to be delivered from the evil influence of the false teachers, and to share his convictions about the truth as it is in Jesus, about the liberty with which Christ has made us free. All Christians should be able to say something like this, especially to unbelievers, namely that we are so satisfied with Jesus Christ, with his freedom, joy, and salvation, that we want other people to become like us.

APPLY

In what areas of your life are you enjoying the freedom of a child of God?

In what areas are you still feeling or behaving like a slave, not in the sense of a servant but in the sense of "bondage to the law, as if your salvation hung in the balance"?

What "weak and miserable forces" of your old life has Christ delivered you from?

PRAY

Pray about your responses above. Ask God to help you in the areas where you face bondage. Let your memories lead you into praise for how he has worked and continues to work in your life.

CELEBRATING FREEDOM

M any people today *want* to be under the law. They are not, of course, the Jews or Judaizers to whom Paul was writing but people whose religion is legalistic, who imagine that the way to God is by the observance of certain rules. There are even professing Christians who turn the gospel into law.

In this passage Paul exposes the inconsistency of their position. This is a difficult allegorical passage, but its message is right up to date.

OPEN

List some of the rules and regulations that Christians imagine will make them acceptable to God.

Why do these "laws" have such a persistent appeal?

STUDY

1. *Read Galatians 4:21-31.* List all the examples of symbolism you note in this passage.

2. What are the contrasts between the two women?

between the two sons?

3. How does Paul use the history of Abraham's two sons, Ishmael and Isaac, to illustrate the supremacy of promise over law? (See Genesis 15–17 and 21:1-21 for background.)

4. How does Paul demonstrate that physical descent from Abraham is not enough to make someone a child of God?

5. Note verse 29. The son born "according to the flesh," Ishmael, would have been seventeen, and Isaac would have been three. What was the conflict between the two sons?

6. Why does conflict persist between followers of the old and new covenants?

An understanding of the Bible is impossible without an understanding of the two covenants. After all, our Bibles are divided in half, into the Old and New Testaments, meaning the Old and New "Covenants." A covenant is a solemn agreement between God and human beings by which he makes them his people and promises to be their God. God established the old covenant through Moses and the new covenant through Christ, whose blood ratified it. The old (Mosaic) covenant was based on law; in it God laid the responsibility on people and said, "Thou shalt . . . , thou shalt not . . ." But the new (Christian) covenant is based on promise; in the promise God keeps the responsibility himself and says, "I will . . . , I will . . ."

7. What is the destiny of those "born according to the flesh" (not born spiritually in Christ)?

8. What are some ways that religious legalists persecute those who have found freedom in Christ?

In this passage there are not only two covenants mentioned but two Jerusalems also. Jerusalem, of course, was the capital city that God chose for the land that he gave to his people. It was natural that the word *Jerusalem* should stand for God's people, just as *Moscow* stands for the Russian people or *Washington* for the people of the United States. But who are the people of God? God's people under the old covenant were the Jews, but his people under the new covenant are Christians, believers. Both are "Jerusalem," but the old covenant people of God, the Jews, are "the present city of Jerusalem," the earthly city, whereas the new covenant people of God, the Christian church, are "the Jerusalem that is above," the heavenly. Thus the two women, Hagar and Sarah, the mothers of Abraham's two sons, stand for the two covenants, the old and the new, and the two Jerusalems, the earthly and the heavenly.

9. What will be the outcome for those who believe God's promises rather than depending on law?

10. In what ways have you seen, or even experienced firsthand, conflict and misunderstanding between legalistic Christians and those who know God's grace and are trusting his promises?

How was it handled and with what outcome?

Summary: The persecution of the true church, of Christian believers who trace their spiritual descent from Abraham, is not always by the world, who are strangers unrelated to us, but by our half-siblings, religious people, the nominal church. The religion of Ishmael is a religion of nature, of what human beings can do by themselves without any special intervention of God. But the religion of Isaac is a religion of grace, of what God has done and does, a religion of divine initiative and divine intervention, for Isaac was born supernaturally through a divine promise. And this is what Christianity is, not natural religion but supernatural. Everyone is either an Ishmael or an Isaac, either still what they are by nature or set free by the grace of God. We must seek to be like Isaac, not like Ishmael. We must put our trust in God through Jesus Christ. Only in Christ can we inherit the promises, receive the grace, and enjoy the freedom of God.

APPLY

How do you usually respond to legalism?

How can "free" Christians guard against their own kind of self-righteousness, feeling superior to legalists?

PRAY

As you praise God for your freedom in Christ, ask him for wisdom to see any pitfalls. Pray for his protection in your spirit and in your relationships.

TRUE AND FALSE RELIGION

GALATIANS 5:1-15

The false teachers in the Galatian churches, as we have already seen, were saying that Christian converts had to be circumcised. You might think this is a very trivial matter. Why did Paul make so much fuss and bother about it? Because of its doctrinal implications. As the false teachers were pressing it, circumcision was neither a physical operation nor a ceremonial rite but a theological symbol. It stood for a particular type of religion, namely salvation by good works in obedience to the law.

Paul answered that you cannot add circumcision (or anything else, for that matter) to Christ as necessary to salvation, because Christ is sufficient for salvation in himself. If you add anything to Christ, you lose Christ. Salvation is in Christ alone by grace alone through faith alone.

OPEN

Different branches of the Christian church practice various ceremonies and observe various scruples according to conscience. How do you discern whether a custom or practice has become elevated to something necessary for salvation?

Speaking in tongues
feet washing
Same Bible

STUDY

1. *Read Galatians 5:1-6.* What is Paul expressing concern about in these verses? *Law vs grace*

2. The freedom described in verse 1 is not primarily a freedom from sin but rather from the law. What Christ has done in liberating us is not so much to set our *will* free from the bondage of sin as to set our *conscience* free from the guilt of sin. What words and phrases throughout this passage indicate what it means to be free?

   Standing firm
   Faith thru love

3. Most people value their freedom very highly. Why would anyone need to be warned to stand fast and avoid submitting to slavery?

   Followers not Leaders

4. How could Jesus Christ ever be said to be "of no value" (v. 2)?

   Dont follow law
   Follow Christ

5. How do you interpret Paul's phrase "fallen away from grace" (v. 4)?

   Fallen from grace
   doesnt mean lose salvation

6. How does Paul's tone change in verses 5 and 6?

   Holy Spirit

7. If we have been declared righteous in Christ, why would Paul say that we still hope for it (v. 5)?

Summary: When a person is in Christ, nothing more is necessary. Neither circumcision nor uncircumcision can improve our standing before God. We wait for our future salvation, the hope of spending eternity with Christ in heaven. We do not work for it; we wait for it by faith.

8. *Read Galatians 5:7-12.* In this section the contrast is between "the one who is throwing you into confusion" (the false teacher) and Paul himself, who is teaching the truth of God. How does the <u>race</u> image highlight the problem?

9. How could Paul be so sure that the "persuasion" of the false teachers was not from God, who had called the Galatians?

10. What is the significance of the "yeast" in the "dough" (v. 9)?

Bad yeast ruins whole batch

11. What was Paul falsely being accused of, and how does he respond (vv. 11-12)?

Preaching anti circumsion

Summary: Paul is quite sure that error is not going to triumph but that the Galatians will come to a better mind and that the false teacher, however exalted his rank, will fall under the judgment of God. Meanwhile Paul was being persecuted. People hate to be told that they can be saved only at the foot of the cross, and they oppose the preacher who tells them so. The good news of Christ crucified is still an offense to human pride. If we preach this gospel, we shall arouse ridicule and opposition. Christianity will not allow us to sit on the fence or live in a haze; it urges us to be definite and decisive, to choose between a religion of human achievement and a religion of divine achievement.

Read Galatians 5:13-15. What sort of freedom is Christian freedom? Primarily it is a freedom of conscience. What Christ has done in liberating us is not so much to set our will free from the bondage of sin as to set our conscience free from the guilt of sin.

12. What are some ways in which the misuse of Christian freedom could lead to self-indulgence?

13. How could freedom degenerate to Christians attacking one another (v. 15)?

14. Why is "love your neighbor as yourself" an appropriate summary of God's law?

Summary: Every single Christian brother and sister has been called by God and called to freedom. It is freedom from the awful bondage of having to merit the favor of God; it is not freedom from all controls. It is a remarkable paradox. For from one point of view Christian freedom is a form of slavery—not slavery to our sinful nature but to our neighbor. We are free in relation to God but slaves in relation to each other.

APPLY

What are your greatest hopes in Christ?

The Judaizers were trying to make circumcision a requirement for salvation. Where are you in the greatest danger of imposing a requirement like the Judaizers? (Consider both positives and negatives—behaviors that Christians "must" do and "must not" do.)

Where are you inclined to indulge yourself in the name of your freedom in Christ?

Who can you serve this week in the freedom of Christian love?

PRAY

Pray for vigilance against misusing your freedom in Christ. Ask God to keep you alert for self-indulgence and for the tendency to condemn others for their freedom.

THE FLESH AND THE SPIRIT

GALATIANS 5:16-25

Internal war. Some teachers maintain that the Christian has no conflict within because (they say) the flesh has been defeated and the old nature is dead. The passage in this study contradicts such a view. According to Martin Luther, Christian people are not "stocks and stones," that is, people who "are never moved with anything, never feel any lust or desires of the flesh" (*Commentary on the Epistle to the Galatians*).

The flesh and the Spirit remain, and the conflict between them is fierce and unremitting. Yet as we learn to walk in the Spirit, the flesh becomes increasingly subdued.

OPEN

For some Christians the Holy Spirit is the vaguest member of the Trinity. For others he is vital to their experience in Christ. How do you see the Holy Spirit in his involvement with your spiritual life?

STUDY

Each time Paul writes of liberty he adds a warning that it can very easily be lost. Some relapse from liberty into bondage (5:1); others turn their liberty into license (5:13). True Christian liberty expresses itself in self-control, loving service of our neighbor, and obedience to the law of God. The question now is this: How are these things possible? And the answer is by the Holy Spirit. He alone can keep us truly free.

Read Galatians 5:16-18. The combatants in the Christian conflict are "the flesh" (in some translations "the sinful nature")—what we are by nature and inheritance, our fallen condition—and "the Spirit"—the Holy Spirit, who renews and regenerates us, first giving us a new nature and then remaining to dwell in us. These two, the flesh and the Spirit, are in sharp opposition to each other.

1. What are the causes of the Christian's inner moral conflict?

2. What are some practical results of the conflict?

3. All Christians have the unhappy experience of discovering that we want God's will but have failed to do it. When we get that insight into ourselves, what are some typical ways we respond?

4. According to this passage, how should we respond to such an insight?

5. How do you interpret the difference between walking by the Spirit (v. 16) and being led by the Spirit (v. 18)?

6. What hope does the promise of verse 16 offer a believer?

Summary: The conflict between the Spirit and the sinful nature is a specifically Christian conflict. There is such a thing as moral conflict in non-Christian people, but it is fiercer in Christians because they possess two natures—flesh and Spirit—in irreconcilable antagonism.

7. *Read Galatians 5:19-25.* What is the root of the contrast between the two ways of living described here?

The acts of the sinful nature are obvious to all. While our old nature itself is secret and invisible, its works, the words and deeds in which it erupts, are public and evident. The sins Paul lists are in the four realms of sex, religion, society, and drink. By contrast, Paul gives a cluster of nine Christian graces, which seem to portray a Christian's attitude to God, to other people, and to self.

8. Consider the areas of sex, religion, society, and drink. Why is each especially vulnerable to corruption by the sinful nature?

9. In Paul's warning to "those who live like this" (v. 21), the Greek verb refers to habitual practice rather than an isolated lapse. Why is the distinction important?

10. Consider the character qualities that are called "the fruit of the Spirit" in verses 22 and 23. What is significant about the fact that they are called "fruit" (in contrast with the "acts" of the sinful nature)?

11. Why is crucifixion (v. 24) an apt description of what must happen to the sinful nature?

12. How do the fruit of the Spirit counteract the destructive effects of the acts of the sinful nature?

13. How do the fruit of the Spirit make us Christlike in our attitude toward God?

toward other people?

toward ourselves?

Summary: If we were left to ourselves, we could not do what we would; instead, we would succumb to the desires of our old nature. But if we "live by the Spirit," then we shall not gratify the desires of the sinful nature. We shall still experience them, but we shall not indulge them. On the contrary, we shall bear the fruit of the Spirit.

APPLY

Which of the acts of the sinful nature are you particularly susceptible to?

Which of the fruit of the Spirit have you sensed in yourself or been told that others see in you?

Which of the fruit of the Spirit do you chronically lack?

How will you choose to live by the Spirit today and the rest of this week?

PRAY

Thank God for his constant grace in Christ, which covers your failures. Thank him also for his protection, which has kept you from many spiritual dangers.

LOVING ONE ANOTHER

GALATIANS 5:26-6:5

The first and great evidence of our walking by the Spirit or being filled with the Spirit is not some private, mystical experience of our own but our practical relationships of love with other people. Since the first fruit of the Spirit is love, this is only logical. But it is easy to talk about "love" in an abstract and general way; it is much harder to get down to concrete, particular situations in which we actually demonstrate our love for one another. It is some of these that Paul now unfolds.

OPEN

How has the Holy Spirit helped you love someone you would otherwise not find very lovable?

STUDY

1. *Read Galatians 5:26–6:5.* In this passage, what positive and negative commands does Paul give the Galatians?

2. Why would conceit lead us to provoke and envy each other (5:26)?

3. How would you describe a person who is spiritual in a Christian sense (6:1)?

4. What temptations accompany seeing another Christian's sin (6:1)?

5. Catching someone in sin would require confrontation, perhaps strong words such as Paul had with Peter (Galatians 2:11). How can gentleness enter into restoration?

6. What does Paul suggest as a cure for pride over another person's falling into sin (6:3)?

Some people think it a sign of fortitude not to bother other people with their burdens. This is more stoical than Christian. It is also true that we should cast all our burdens on Jesus Christ, since he cares for us. But one of the ways in which Jesus bears these burdens of ours is through human friendship.

7. When is it hard for you to ask others for help (6:2)?

8. How can Paul say a Christian is "nothing" (6:3)?

9. What are some practical steps we can take to test our own actions (6:4)?

10. Pride is not usually considered a Christian characteristic. What sort of pride is Paul talking about in verse 4?

11. What dangers are inherent in comparing ourselves with others (6:4)?

12. Verse 2 tells us to carry each other's burdens, while verse 5 says we have to carry our own loads. The Greek word in verse 2 means a weight or heavy load, while the Greek word in verse 5 is a common term for a person's pack. So there is no contradiction. We are to bear one another's burdens, which are too heavy for each of us to bear alone, but we cannot share the burden of our own responsibility to God. What are some examples of burdens that Christians can and should carry for each other?

What sorts of burdens should not be shared?

13. Reconsider the fruit of the Spirit from study ten (Galatians 5:22-23). In this passage, which of them is Paul calling on the Galatians to exercise?

Summary: Truly Christian relationships are governed not by rivalry but by service. The correct attitude is not "I'm better than you, and I'll prove it" but "You are a person of importance in your own right (because God made you in his own image and Christ died for you), and it is my joy and privilege to serve you." If we walked by the Spirit, we would love one another more, and if we loved one another more, we would bear one another's burdens, and if we bore one another's burdens, we would not shrink from seeking to restore a Christian who has fallen into sin. By such practical Christian living, the law of Christ is fulfilled.

APPLY

To love one another as Christ loved us may lead us not to some heroic, spectacular deed of self-sacrifice but to the much more mundane and unspectacular ministry of burden-bearing. When we see somebody with a heavy burden on the heart or mind, we must be ready to get alongside that person and share the burden. Similarly, we must be humble enough to let others share ours.

What burdens of your own do you need to share with others?

Whose burdens can you help carry today?

PRAY

Who do you know who needs to be restored in the sense Paul used here? Pray for that person and what part God might want you to have in restoring them.

Think of someone you tend to provoke and someone you tend to envy. How might conceit be involved in your responses to those people? Pray for understanding into your own heart.

SOWING AND REAPING

W e reap what we sow. If we are faithful and conscientious in our sowing, then we can confidently expect a good harvest. If we "sow wild oats," as we sometimes say, then we must not expect to reap straw-berries! On the contrary, "those who plough evil / and those who sow trouble reap it" (Job 4:8).

In this final section of Galatians Paul has a few final admonitions. At first sight, these instructions and exhortations appear to be very loosely connected, even totally disconnected. But the connecting link is the great principle of sowing and reaping, the principle of order and consistency that is written into all life, material and moral.

OPEN

When have you seen "good sowing" produce "good reaping"?

STUDY

Read Galatians 6:6-10. If farmers want a bumper harvest of a particular grain, then they must sow not only the right seed but good seed and that plentifully. Only if they do this can they expect a good crop. Precisely the same principle operates in the moral and spiritual sphere. It is not the reapers who decide what the harvest is going to be like but the sowers.

1. What various contrasts does Paul draw in this passage?

2. How does verse 6 apply to people in the Christian ministry and those who benefit from their ministry?

3. What are some ways that people imagine they can mock God (v. 7)?

4. Verse 8 is obviously not talking about literal seed. Then what sorts of things are "sown"?

5. What are some examples of both bad and good reaping (v. 8)?

6. What are some ways that we can get tired from doing good (v. 9)?

7. Why should "the family of believers" deserve our special attention (v. 10)?

Summary: We are not the helpless victims of our nature, temperament, and environment. On the contrary, what we become depends largely on how we behave; our character is shaped by our conduct. How can we expect to reap the fruit of the Spirit if we do not sow in the field of the Spirit? Holiness is a harvest; whether we reap it or not depends almost entirely on what and where we sow.

Read Galatians 6:11-18. Now Paul takes the pen from his secretary's hand in order to add a personal postscript. His "large letters" may actually refer to his handwriting, or the phrase may mean that Paul wants to especially emphasize what he is going to say next. The vital issues at stake are two questions: Is the essence of the Christian religion outward or inward? And is it human or divine—fundamentally a matter of what we do for God or of what he has done for us?

8. How did Paul appraise the motives of the Judaizers who insisted on circumcision (vv. 12-13)?

9. How would outward keeping of the law avoid persecution for the cross (v. 12)?

10. How could Paul "boast" in the cross of Christ (v. 14)?

11. What are some examples of "outward" religion that people mistake for true Christianity?

12. How can the church experience peace and mercy (v. 16)?

Summary: It is natural for fallen humanity to decline from the real, the inward, and the spiritual and to fabricate a substitute religion that is easy and comfortable because its demands are external and ceremonial only. But outward things matter little in comparison with the new creation or the new birth.

APPLY

In your own experience, what outward signs or works are you tempted to substitute for inner spiritual reality?

Consider accomplishments you are tempted to boast about. How can you turn those around and give credit to Christ?

PRAY

Praise God for making you a new creation in Jesus Christ. Pray that your life in Christ will take precedence over everything else.

GUIDELINES FOR LEADERS

MY GRACE IS SUFFICIENT FOR YOU.
2 CORINTHIANS 12:9

I f leading a small group is something new for you, don't worry. These sessions are designed to be led easily. Because the Bible study questions flow from observation to interpretation to application, you may feel as if the studies lead themselves.

You don't need to be an expert on the Bible or a trained teacher to lead a small group discussion. As a leader, you can guide group members to discover for themselves what the Bible has to say and to listen for God's guidance. This method of learning will allow group members to remember much more of what is said than a lecture would.

This study guide is flexible. You can use it with a variety of groups—students, professionals, neighborhood, or church groups. Each study takes forty-five to sixty minutes in a group setting.

There are some important facts to know about group dynamics and encouraging discussion. The following suggestions should equip you to effectively and enjoyably fulfill your role as leader.

PREPARING FOR THE STUDY

1. Ask God to help you understand and apply the passage in your own life. Unless this happens, you will not be prepared to lead others. Pray, too, for the various members of the group. Ask God to open your hearts to the message of his Word and motivate you to action.

2. Read the introduction to the entire guide to get an overview of the topics that will be explored.

3. As you begin each study, read and reread the assigned Bible passage to familiarize yourself with it.

4. This study guide is based on the New International Version of the Bible. It will help you and the group if you use this translation as the basis for your study and discussion. The New Revised Standard Version is also recommended.

5. Carefully work through each question in the study. Spend time in meditation and reflection as you consider how to respond.

6. Write your thoughts and responses in the space provided in the study guide. This will help you to express your understanding of the passage clearly.

7. It may help to have a Bible dictionary handy. Use it to look up any unfamiliar words, names, or places. (For additional help on how to study a passage, see *How to Lead a LifeGuide Bible Study* from Inter-Varsity Press.)

8. Take the "Apply" portion of each study seriously. Consider how you need to apply the Scripture to your life. Remember that the group members will follow your lead in responding to the studies. They will not go any deeper than you do.

LEADING THE STUDY

1. Begin the study on time. Open with prayer, asking God to help the group to understand and apply the passage.

2. Be sure that everyone in your group has a study guide. Encourage the group to prepare beforehand for each discussion by reading the introduction to the guide and by working through the questions in each study.

3. At the beginning of your first time together, explain that these studies are meant to be discussions, not lectures. Encourage the members of the group to participate. However, do not put pressure on those who may be hesitant to speak during the first few sessions.

4. Have a group member read aloud the introduction at the beginning of the discussion.

5. Every session begins with an "open" question, which is meant to be asked before the passage is read. These questions are designed to introduce the theme of the study and encourage group members to begin to open up. Encourage as many members as possible to participate, and be ready to get the discussion going with your own response. These opening questions can reveal where our thoughts or feelings need to be transformed by Scripture. That is why it is especially important not to read the passage before the question is asked. The passage will tend to color the honest reactions people would otherwise give because they are, of course, supposed to think the way the Bible does.

6. Have a group member read aloud the passage to be studied.

7. As you ask the study questions, keep in mind that they are designed to be used just as they are written. You may simply read them aloud. Or you may prefer to express them in your own words.

    There may be times when it is appropriate to deviate from the study guide. For example, a question may have already been answered. If so, move on to the next question. Or someone may raise an important question not covered in the guide. Take time to discuss it, but try to keep the group from going on tangents.

8. Avoid answering your own questions. If necessary, repeat or rephrase them until they are clearly understood. Or point the group to the commentary woven into the guide to clarify the context or meaning *without answering the question*. An eager group quickly becomes passive and silent if members think the leader will do most of the talking.

9. Don't be afraid of silence in response to the discussion questions. People may need time to think about the question before formulating their answers.

10. Don't be content with just one answer. Ask, "What do the rest of you think?" or "Anything else?" until several people have given answers to the question.

11. Acknowledge all contributions. Try to be affirming whenever possible. Never reject an answer. If it is clearly off-base, ask, "Which verse led you to that conclusion?" or again, "What do the rest of you think?"

12. Don't expect every answer to be addressed to you, even though this will probably happen at first. As group members become more at ease, they will begin to truly interact with each other. This is one sign of healthy discussion.

13. Don't be afraid of controversy. It can be very stimulating. If you don't resolve an issue completely, don't be frustrated. Explain that the group will move on and God may enlighten all of you in later sessions.

14. Periodically summarize what the group has said about the passage. This helps to draw together the various ideas mentioned and gives continuity to the study. But don't preach.

15. Conclude your time together with conversational prayer, adapting the prayer suggestion at the end of the study to your group. Ask for God's help in following through on the commitments you've made.

16. End on time.

Many more suggestions and helps can be found in *How to Lead a Life-Guide Bible Study* and *The Big Book on Small Groups* (both from Inter-Varsity Press) or *Housegroups* (Crossway Books, UK). Reading through one of these books would be worth your time.

ALSO AVAILABLE

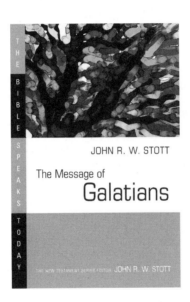

THE BIBLE SPEAKS TODAY

JOHN R. W. STOTT

The Message of
Galatians

THE NEW TESTAMENT SERIES EDITOR: JOHN R. W. STOTT

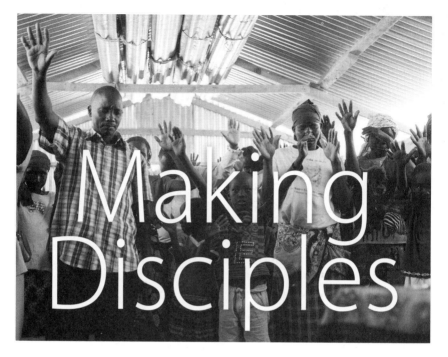

Around the World — Christianity is exploding with growth in numbers

Yet — Believers are struggling to grow in Christ

That's Why Langham Exists

Our Vision

To see churches in the Majority World equipped for mission and growing to maturity in Christ through the ministry of pastors and leaders who believe, teach and live by the Word of God.

www.langham.org

FOUNDED BY JOHN STOTT

Langham®
PARTNERSHIP